the *Filipino* cookbook

85 Homestyle Recipes to Delight Your Family and Friends

Miki Garcia

Photos by **Luca Invernizzi Tettoni**

Styling by **Theo Domini O. Zaragoza**

TUTTLE Publishing

contents

Roasted Marinated Pork (page 46)

Filipino Cooking:
Asia's Best-kept Culinary Secret

My adventure with Filipino cooking began when I lived in Manila and in rural Iba (in Zambales Province) for about a year in the 1990s. I had always loved the country and the people of these tropical islands; however, it was only after living there for several years that I discovered and grew to love the amazing variety of foods that the Philippines has to offer. When I met and later married my Filipino husband, my love of the cuisine was further strengthened since he was from the province of Pampanga in Central Luzon, which is considered by most Filipinos to have some of the best cooking in the nation.

Kapampangans—as the people from Pampanga are called in Filipino—are skilled cooks and spend a great deal of their time preparing fine dishes and sharing sumptuous meals with relatives and friends. When not cooking, the Kapampangans are generally thinking about what to prepare for their next meal. This great passion for food and attention to detail means that my husband loves to spend time in the kitchen, and even when I am cooking he likes to interrupt me and often offers to take over, especially if he feels I'm not doing things correctly the "Kapampangan way." Due to this, I can truly say that his Kapampangan food culture has thoroughly rubbed off on me over the years.

Even though we have lived in many other countries of Asia and Europe and now live in America, I prefer to cook Filipino dishes whenever we entertain because I find that everybody loves the food. Over the years I have scribbled enough recipes to fill up several notebooks. For many years, I tried to find a cookbook of Kapampangan and other regional Filipino recipes that would satisfy the discriminating tastes of our Filipino friends and relatives, but I could never find one. I ended up asking my foodie friends and relatives for their favorite recipes, trying them out whenever I could, and, through trial and error, compiling a large collection of recipes that seem to exemplify the best dishes and flavors from all parts of the archipelago. Thus, this cookbook, the result of that effort, reflects the very best of Filipino cooking, and the recipes encompass a large selection of traditional and authentic dishes that can be enjoyed by anyone on any occasion and are accessible to Filipinos and non-Filipinos alike.

Filipino cuisine is one of the best-kept culinary secrets in Asia. Unlike Japanese, Chinese or Thai food, its dishes are not readily available in restaurants. Filipinos love to entertain in large groups and have a tradition of throwing large and loud parties at home. And so it is only in Filipino homes—wherever they are around the world—that can one find truly authentic Filipino cuisine.

Like other cuisines, Filipino cooking reveals a great deal about the history and geography of the place from which it sprang and the people who created it. The dishes were not developed in the kitchens of royal palaces or by wealthy aristocrats, and nor is there a long tradition of dining out in restaurants. The food is instead the creation of the common folk. In short, Filipino cuisine is the everyday "people's food." Its dishes are prepared to be enjoyed by everyone whenever there is a reason or occasion to gather and celebrate. Filipinos view food primarily as a means of connecting with family and friends rather than an end in itself.

One of the things I love about Filipino cuisine is its simplicity. By and large, the dishes do not require any special utensils, there are no complicated techniques, and it does not use many exotic or expensive ingredients. Most of all, preparation times are short since it's often too hot and humid in the Philippines to spend very much time in the kitchen!

The ingredients required to make Filipino dishes are, for the most part, very easy to find. Expatriate Filipino communities, and markets catering to their needs, have sprung up in many urban areas around the world. In addition, a large number of Filipino ingredients originally came from the New World (brought over by the Spanish from Mexico) and can now be found in most large and well-stocked supermarkets (see pages 12–17 for a list of Essential Filipino Ingredients).

The Filipino national cuisine is an amalgamation of many different regional styles from the various islands as well as many historical influences from abroad. The Filipinos themselves describe their cuisine as *sari-sari* (varied) and *halo-halo* (mixed) because of the wide array of influences found even within a single meal. Filipino cooking can truly be considered a melting pot, deeply influenced by over 100 different island ethnic groups as well as by settlers from all parts of Asia, and by the Spanish and American colonizers.

The native inhabitants of the islands are known as Aetas, who still live in the mountains of Luzon and Mindanao. They are believed to share the same ancestry as the aboriginals of Australia and the Papuans of New Guinea. The arrival of the Malayo-Polynesian peoples from the Asian mainland via Taiwan 6,000 years ago drove them into the mountains, and

Malayo-Polynesians are now the predominant inhabitants of the Philippines. Their cooking styles involve the preparation of foods by boiling, roasting and steaming using coconut milk and peanut oil. The roasting of a whole pig, known as Lechon, is believed to be an ancient Polynesian practice.

Regular contacts with the Chinese also influenced Filipino cuisine. Chinese traders, who visited and settled on the islands from the fifth century onward, brought their culinary techniques and ingredients. Fried Rice Noodles (page 93) and Spring Rolls (page 31) are two typical Filipino dishes with their roots in China. Many of the typical Filipino *sawsawan*, or dipping sauces, are also of Chinese origin. Prior to the arrival of the Spanish, the islands were also visited by Arab, Japanese, Thai, Vietnamese, Javanese, Cambodian, Indian and Portuguese traders. Each of these cultures subtly influenced the evolution of the local cuisine.

The Spanish colonization of the Philippines in the sixteenth century lasted for 300 years and brought significant Spanish and Mexican influence, via Spain's colonization of that country, to the food culture of the islands. Located on the vital sea routes of Asia, the Philippines became a lucrative trading port for the Spanish. In exchange for sugar and other local products, the Spanish brought chili peppers, tomatoes, corn, cacao and potatoes from the New World. It is said that as many as 80 percent of local Filipino dishes have some Spanish or Mexican influence, either because of their ingredients or because they are local adaptations of original Spanish or Mexican dishes.

Many Chinese dishes that were introduced during the Spanish colonial times were given Spanish names. For example, the ever-popular Chinese rice congee was given the name Arroz Caldo (Rice Porridge with Chicken, page 92), while Chinese-style fried rice was called Morisqueta Tostada—commonly known by its Tagalog name, Sinangag (Fried Rice with Egg, page 91). Spanish food and culture, and the Catholic religion, continue to define the modern-day Philippines even though Spanish colonial rule ended in 1898.

Sautéed Squid (page 70)

Following the Spanish-American War, these islands fell under the spell of American culture during a time of rapid modernization. American-made canned foods became widely available and people used them to create new dishes. Canned meats and sausages became popular staples as did canned fruit cocktails and condensed milk. Karne Norte, for example, is a popular dish consisting of canned corned beef sautéed with garlic and onions, and Halo-Halo is a delicious dessert of shaved ice with sweet syrups and canned evaporated milk. The Philippine-American experience gave the Filipinos many new ways of turning foreign food influences into something delicious and uniquely Filipino.

Regional Cooking Styles

In addition to these foreign influences, the geography of the Philippines has also contributed to the diversity of its cuisine. As an archipelago comprising of 7,107 islands and seventeen regions, 120 different ethnic groups and 170 different languages, the formation of regional cooking styles is inevitable. Regional traditions, preferences, and available ingredients can transform a dish into something entirely different as one travels from one end of the archipelago to the other. To give you a sense of the richness of Filipino diversity in its cuisine, this book includes the best recipes from these various regions—from the rugged north shores of the Ilocos region to the southern island of Mindanao.

On the northwest coast of Luzon, between the mountains and the sea, is the Ilocos region. Here, the land is rugged and dry. In this harsh climate, the Ilocano people survive by being frugal and hardworking. Ilocano meals include an abundance of vegetables with some type of meat as the main feature of the meal. Ilocanos prepare their vegetables by steaming or boiling them with a dash of sautéed fermented shrimp paste. Red meat dishes are not commonly found, but freshwater fish are featured prominently. Their signature vegetable dish, Pinakbet (Mixed Vegetables with Anchovy Sauce, page 80), includes plenty of locally grown vegetables like bitter gourd, okra, and eggplant served with a tasty anchovy sauce.

Pampanga has a well-earned reputation as the home to the most creative and refined cuisines found in the Philippines. Located in the central part of Luzon just east of Manila, Pampanga's fertile soils and fish-filled rivers give the region the necessary ingredients to build its well-deserved reputation. Spanish chefs provided the Kapampangans with just enough guidance on European cooking techniques to enable them to create their own unique and delectable native dishes. Soon these dishes would outshine their European equivalents on the tables of Spanish royalty (it was the Kapampangans who prepared the meal at the proclamation of the first Philippine Republic). Among the original Kapampangan recipes featured in this book are Kaldereta Beef Stew (page 53), Oxtail Vegetable Stew (page 56), Traditional Tocino Bacon (page 50), Chicken Tamales (page 28), Kapampangan Paella (page 89), and Filipino Leche Flan (page 108).

The Bicol region is located at the southern tail of the Luzon peninsula, and includes some of the surrounding small islands. A part of the "Ring of Fire," it has several volcanoes whose lava flows provide the region with its fertile and lush green landscape. Possessing an ideal climate for coconut trees, the region is one of the major coconut-producing provinces in the Philippines, and so their dishes often include coconut ingredients. Coconut milk, for instance, is cooked with virtually everything—vegetables, meat, and seafood. Their signature dish, Bicol Express (Fiery Pork Stew with Coconut, page 49) is pork simmered in coconut milk with a generous helping of spicy peppers (Bicolanos are famous for using hot peppers to liven up their regional dishes).

The Visayas region of the Philippines consists of a group of islands that draws upon the abundance of the sea to create its cuisines. I've included Visayan dishes like Filipino Ceviche (Kinilaw na Tanigue, page 77), which is fish marinated in vinegar and then eaten raw—a typically Visayan way to enjoy fresh seafood from the local waters. This is a region with a large population of Chinese settlers, so there is a range of Chinese-influenced specialties, such as Wonton Soup (page 37) and Noodle Soup with All the Trimmings (Batchoy, page 40), reflecting that influence.

At the southeastern end of the archipelago is the second largest Filipino island, Mindanao. It was here that Muslims from Indonesia and Malaysia converted the people to the religion of Islam. When the Spaniards arrived, they were unable to completely dominate the island due to the resistance of its recently established Muslim religion. This separatist attitude has

flavored the development of Mindanao's culture and cuisine. Mindanao offers a wide range of exotic dishes, and, though Christians form the majority of the population of Mindanao today, the Islamic religion continues to be a dominant influence on this island's cuisines (pork dishes, for example, are hardly present). Their distinct chicken curry is simmered with taro roots in a very spicy sauce and served with rice. Mindanao food, especially the Sulu and Tawi-Tawi Islands, is renowned for its use of spices such as turmeric, cumin, lemongrass, coriander, and chilis. In this warm climate, spices help keep food from spoiling while lending richness to the dishes.

As one travels through the Philippines, each of the dishes encountered reflects the character and spirit of the people who live there. The Filipino people have a loyalty and devotion to their home regions matched only by a feeling of national pride borne from centuries of foreign rule.

Foods for Celebrations

Filipinos love to celebrate! Throughout the year they will find any excuse to hold a feast in order to prepare delicious foods and socialize with friends and family. Of all the annual events that are an occasion to celebrate, the most conspicuous event of the year is the town festival called *fiesta* in honor of the town's Catholic patron saint. As a result of almost four hundred years of work by Catholic missionaries, the Philippines is the largest Catholic country in Asia and Filipinos have embraced their Catholic beliefs and customs, especially the annual fiesta.

The day's festivities start at the crack of dawn, when a band plays music while walking the streets of the town, awakening the whole village. Richly embroidered tablecloths are spread and tables are set in preparation for the day's feast. The culinary centerpiece of the celebration is the beloved Lechon, a whole pig stuffed with rice and roasted slowly over a charcoal pit. The sight of this distinctly Filipino fiesta food will immediately conjure mouthwatering childhood memories for all adult Filipinos.

Another time for food and celebration is All Souls' Day when Filipinos visit cemeteries to pay respects to their deceased loved ones. All through the night of November 1st, Filipinos eat, sing, and gossip—while large amounts of food and drink are passed around and over tombstones. This same celebratory ethos applies to funerals, where refreshments are provided for everyone in attendance and there is a sense of communal gaiety. Typical meals eaten on these days are Pig Blood Stew (Dinuguan), Steamed Rice Cakes and Sautéed Bean Thread Noodles (page 95).

The biggest national Philippine celebration is *Pasko*, or Christmas. Filipinos do not confine the celebration to December but will start as early as September when they begin hanging Christmas lights and singing Christmas carols. They even continue the celebration past Christmas and make the first Sunday of January the official end to their holiday reveling. From the 16th of December through Christmas Eve, Filipinos celebrate *Simbang Gabi*, a Filipino version of *Misa de Gallo* (Mass of the Rooster), a nine-day celebration held at four in the morning on each day. An integral part of Simbang Gabi is the availability of refreshments from local street vendors. Sleepy and hungry churchgoers can enjoy Coconut Sponge Cakes (Bibingka, page 103), Purple Rice Cakes with Coconut Shavings (Puto Bumbong), Chicken Tamales (page 28), Filipino Hot Chocolate (page 105) and Healthy Ginger Tea (Salabat, page 107) as a part of the celebration. As Christmas Eve becomes Christmas morning, family members gather to share a festive *Noche Buena* meal of Glazed Christmas Ham with Pineapple (Hamon, page 49), cheese, lechon, Spring Rolls (Lumpiang Shanghai, page 31), Fried Rice Noodles (Pancit Guisado, page 93), Barbequed Chicken Skewers (page 61), Fruit Salad, Chicken Macaroni Salad, and other dishes.

Finally, New Year's Eve provides another chance for family to gather around a table of celebratory foods. This meal is called the *Media Noche* and is served just before midnight strikes. Filipinos believe that plenty of food on the table means a year of plenty for everyone in the family. Twelve different fruits, especially round ones like grapes and *chicos* (or *sapodilla*, a brown berry with a sweet and malty taste) that resemble money, are displayed to invite prosperity for the coming year. Other Filipinos believe that eating twelve grapes on New Year's Eve will ensure a year of good luck.

If all of this isn't enough, many Filipinos get married in the months of December and January providing yet one more reason to cook large amounts of food and gather together with family and friends for a celebration. Essentially, Filipinos love any reason to eat and enjoy each other's company!

How to Eat a Filipino Meal

Most Filipinos prefer to eat with their hands, especially in informal situations. Making sure their hands are clean, Filipinos always use the fingers of their right hand (even left-handed diners) to take a small portion of rice and to press it into a mound. A piece of meat, fish, or vegetable is placed on top of this mound and picked up with the fingers, and then brought to the mouth where the thumb is used to push the food into the mouth. It might take some practice, but this is the authentic way of eating Filipino food.

The Spanish introduced forks and spoons and, since then, their use has become widespread. The fork is normally held in the left hand and the spoon in the right hand. A knife is not normally needed since most foods are either pre-cut into bite-sized pieces or tender enough to be cut using the spoon. The spoon is used to collect and then scoop up a mouthful of food while the fork keeps it from moving off the plate. Only in the most formal settings will you see a knife used. Although the Chinese left a lasting impression on Filipino food and culture, chopsticks are generally not used. Filipinos use a flat plate, making it impractical to pick up rice with chopsticks.

Another unique part of the Filipino dining experience is the use of *patis* (fish sauce) and *bagoong* (either sautéed shrimp paste or anchovy sauce) as condiments. These condiments (*pampalasa)* are used in soups, stews, and to accompany just about any dish on the Filipino table. Even when a dish is flavorful and well seasoned, a Filipino will still want to add patis or bagoong. So remember to put a small saucer or patis or bagoong on the table during mealtime if you want to keep your Filipino guests happy.

Meals are served family style—that is, they are placed in the center of the table with individual serving spoons, allowing each diner to take only the desired portion. *Viands* —the dishes that accompany rice—mostly have bite-sized slices of meat and vegetables.

Filipinos are easygoing and hospitable. They love to share their food! If you are visiting a Filipino home, you will definitely be offered helpings of local specialties—and if it's fiesta time, you'll enjoy even more.

Guests are treated with respect, but don't start to eat until the host says so. Don't hesitate to take a second or third helping as your host will be delighted that you're enjoying the dishes. If you don't like the food, try to eat a little bit out of courtesy. It is always important for guests to accept food offered by the host or fellow guests—never decline! Make sure you finish everything on your plate; otherwise the hostess will think you didn't appreciate her cooking. Above all, enjoy the hospitality of family and friends while sampling the variety of textures and tastes found in Filipino cuisine.

Fried Rice Noodles (page 93)

Essential Filipino Ingredients

Filipino ingredients can be found in Asian or Latin American grocery stores. If there are Filipino eateries in your neighborhood, it is worth checking with them to find out where they get their supplies. Chinatowns are also good places to look. Many hard-to-find fresh vegetables, such as bitter gourd, can be found frozen, canned, or bottled. Also, a wide variety of Filipino products are now available from online businesses (see Resources, page 112).

Agar-Agar is a thickening agent made from seaweed that is used to make desserts and jellies. It is flavorless and dissolves when boiled in water and sets to a gelatinous form when left to cool. It is similar to gelatin although gelatin is made from animal by-products and easily dissolves in hot water. Agar-agar gels more firmly than gelatin too. Known as *gulaman* in the Philippines, agar-agar is sold as dried white or colored bars or packed as flakes or powder. Look for them in Asian or health food stores.

Anchovy Sauce, or *bagoong isda*, is fermented fish sauce—anchovies are commonly used—that is popular either as an ingredient or condiment. Anchovy sauce is very salty, has a strong, pungent smell, and varies in appearance, color, and flavor. No need to sauté or cook the sauce when used as a condiment. Asian groceries sell bottles of gray-colored anchovy sauce either as *bagoong monamon* or *bagoong balayan*, and may contain whole anchovies. Do not confuse with regular fish sauce or *patis*. See also Sautéed Shrimp Paste.

Annatto Seeds are tiny, dried reddish-brown seeds used as natural food coloring. They have little flavor and are mainly added to impart a tinge of red color to dishes. The seed is usually soaked and squeezed in warm water or fried in oil to extract the reddish orange color (see How to Make Annatto Water, page 19). The seed is from the annatto fruit, originally brought from Mexico to the Philippines. It is sold in packets or bottles in Asian or Latin American grocery stores. Mixing paprika with ground turmeric powder is a good substitute. Red food coloring may also be used, or you can simply omit the coloring agent altogether.

Bananas Among many varieties, *saba* bananas are widely cultivated in the Philippines. They are shorter in length but stouter than regular bananas. The skins are thick and green when unripe, yellow when ripe. In a typical Filipino dish, unripe or semi-ripe saba bananas are used. Semi-ripe or ripe saba bananas are fried, grilled, and boiled for desserts and soups. Saba bananas are usually cut into four pieces when used in

soups. Thinner slices are called for in desserts such as Sweet Coconut Milk Delight (page 98) and Mixed Fruits and Shaved Ice Parfait (Halo-halo, page 104). Frozen saba bananas are available in Asian grocery stores. Plantains or unripe regular bananas may be substituted (use about half of a plantain for every saba banana.)

Banana Blossom Also known as banana flower or banana heart (*puso ng saging* is the term commonly used in the Philippines, *puso* is Filipino for heart), this vegetable is an edible bud from the banana plant and is actually several layers of reddish fibrous skins. Fresh, bottled, or canned banana blossoms are sold in Asian grocery stores. When using a fresh blossom, remove several layers of the hard outer sheets to reveal the lighter-colored inner layers, cut into thin circles or quarters, and soak them in salted water before cooking. Artichoke hearts or zucchini flowers may be used as substitutes.

Banana Ketchup looks just like regular ketchup and is made from bananas, tomatoes, sugar, vinegar, and spices. It has a sweet-and-sour taste and doesn't taste like bananas at all. The red coloring is added so it looks like tomato ketchup. Banana ketchup is cheaper than tomato ketchup in the Philippines, and is also commonly found in Hawaii and the West Indies. It is often used as a dip for fried chicken, hotdogs, and other fried dishes. It is readily available in Asian grocery stores. Tomato ketchup is a good substitute.

Banana Leaves are sold either as large sheets folded up, or pre-cut to smaller sizes. These versatile leaves can be baked, grilled, used as a cooking sheet, a plate, or a wrapper for steamed dishes. The banana leaf gives the food a nice texture, color, and taste. Leaves should be rinsed, cut, and held over an open flame for a few seconds or scalded with boiling water to "wilt" them and make them easy to fold without cracking. The leaves can also make a beautiful and exotic background when used as serving plates and party platters. Frozen leaves are often sold in large sizes and can be cut down to smaller sizes. Leftover leaves can be simply wrapped in plastic and stored in the freezer. They are available either fresh or frozen in Asian or Latin American grocery stores. Aluminum foil can be used as a substitute.

Bitter Gourd, or bitter melon, is a very nutritious vegetable—it controls blood sugar levels—but has a warty exterior and bitter taste that can be off-putting to some. To remove the bitter taste, slice the gourd in small pieces and then soak them in warm salted water, or lightly boil in salted water before cooking. The skin is edible but you need to discard the spongy interior and seeds. When it is ripe, it becomes more bitter; the skin turns yellowish and the seeds become red. With its distinct taste, it is difficult to find a substitute. Fresh, frozen, canned, and bottled bitter gourd is available in Asian and Latin American grocery stores. Canned or bottled bitter gourd is widely available at online grocery stores (see Resources, page 112).

Calamansi Limes are smaller than regular limes. They are round and grow on small bushes all over the Philippines. The juice has a milder and more fragrant taste than regular lime juice. Calamansi limes are halved and usually squeezed over noodles or just about any dish, and are used in marinades or in dipping sauces mixed with soy sauce and chili. Bottled calamansi concentrate can be found in Asian grocery stores, but it is normally sweetened and used mainly for drinks. If fresh calamansi is not available, substitute lime or lemon.

Cane Vinegar (*suka*) is a very important ingredient of Filipino cooking. Along with salt, vinegar was used to keep food from spoiling without refrigeration in hot and humid Philippines so most, if not all, dishes are salted and use vinegar. Throughout this cookbook, mild cane vinegar is used. It is often labeled *sukang maasim* or "sour vinegar." Any Philippine-made palm vinegar (*sukang paombong*) or coconut vinegar (*sukang niyog*) can be substituted. Filipino vinegar is less acidic than most vinegars used in the West. The best substitutes are white vinegar, white wine vinegar, or cider vinegar. However, if you use these vinegars they should be diluted with water (use 3 parts vinegar to 1 part water).

Chayote is a light green pear-shaped vegetable that comes from Mexico. It belongs to the squash family and the taste is like zucchini or summer squash. It should be peeled and deseeded. When buying, try to find chayotes that are firm and without spots. It is often a substitute for green papaya in dishes such as Chicken Soup with Green Papaya (page 42).

Finger-length green chilies

Bird's-eye chilies

Chili Peppers Bird's-eye chilies, or *siling labuyo,* refer to the small, hot peppers that are usually finely chopped and mixed with vinegar and soy sauce to make dipping sauces. Finger-length green chilies, or *siling mahaba,* are long, thin and flat and are commonly used in stews and soups. *Siling bilog* refers to bell peppers.

Chinese Cabbage (Napa cabbage) is also known as snow cabbage, *pak choi,* or Peking cabbage. Unlike European cabbage, it has an elongated head with white stalks and green leaves. It is rich in Vitamin C, fiber, and folic acid, and widely available in supermarkets.

Chorizo de Bilbao are dried sausages that originally came from the Basque province of Spain. The Philippine version of *chorizo* is more like a Chinese sausage—spicy, firm, and dry-cured. It is similar to salami with a salty-and-sweet flavor. It is more popular than fresh sausages because it stores well for a longer period at room temperature. It is available in vacuum packs in the unrefrigerated sections of Asian or Latin American grocery stores. A good substitute is any dried, sweet sausage or Chinese *lap cheong* sausages, which are found in vacuum packs in the frozen section. Chorizo de Bilbao should be refrigerated after opening.

Coconut Sport Strings are the sliced meat of a variety of coconut palm fruit called *macapuno* that does not contain water inside the shell. It looks exactly the same as a regular coconut, but the meat is softer, making it ideal for desserts. It can be used as toppings for Sweet Purple Yam Pudding (page 99) or Mixed Fruits and Shaved Ice Parfait (Halo-halo, page 104). Jars and cans of it are sold in Asian grocery stores.

Grated Coconut is sold fresh in markets in Asia, and you can buy bags of it frozen in some Asian grocery stores. You can also buy brown husked coconuts, crack them open, remove the flesh and grate it in a blender although it's a lot of work. Another solution is to use unsweetened dried grated coconut and add water to reconstitute it.

Coconut Milk comes in two types: thick and thin. To obtain thick coconut milk, place about 3 cups (600 g) of fresh grated coconut (the amount that one coconut yields) and 1/2 cup (125 ml) of warm water in a bowl, knead for 3 minutes, place in a cloth and squeeze. Thick milk is best for desserts. To obtain thin coconut milk, add 1 cup (250 ml) of water to the same grated coconut, place in a cheesecloth and squeeze. Thin milk is used for general cooking. Use fresh coconut milk immediately as any leftover gets spoiled easily. Canned coconut milk is widely available and the thickness varies depending on the brand. Once opened, coconut milk should be kept refrigerated and stored only for a couple of days; otherwise, it begins to sour. You can freeze it but thaw fully before cooking.

Fermented Black Beans (*tausi*) Also called "salted black beans," tausi has a pungent, bitter, and salty flavor. Tausi is sold in jars in most Asian grocery stores.

Filipino Cane Vinegar *See* Cane Vinegar

Fish Sauce (*patis*) is a very salty, translucent, amber-colored, fermented sauce that is usually available in tall bottles under various brand names. It is very salty so it does not require refrigeration and will keep indefinitely. As an essential ingredient in Filipino dishes, fish sauce is either used as a

seasoning when cooking or used as a dipping sauce. Fish sauces made in Vietnam, Thailand and China are very similar and may be used in place of Filipino fish sauce.

Fried Pork Rinds (*chicharon*) are crunchy, deep-fried and seasoned pork skins that are dipped in spicy vinegar, crushed and used as toppings or as an ingredient in soups and stews. There are different types of chicharon available from various Spanish-speaking countries. Look for Filipino chicharon if you can, or buy the thin pork cracklings without flavoring. They are sold in bags in Asian or Latin American grocery stores.

Green Papaya is the unripe papaya fruit. It has a green skin, white meat, and tiny white seeds that is most often used like a vegetable. If not available, chayote is a good substitute.

Glutinous Rice (*malagkit*) in the Philippines is used for *kakanin*—sweet rice desserts like Sweet Rice Cakes with Fried Coconut Topping (page 100) or Rice Cakes with Sweet Coconut Filling (page 109) or for Kapampangan Paella (page 89). This type of rice turns sticky when cooked. It is sold in bags in Asian food stores and many supermarkets.

Jackfruit (*langka*) is native to India, and is the largest tree-borne fruit in the world. The tree itself reaches up to 60 feet (18 m)

Canton

Cornstarch Noodles

Mami

Misua

Mung Bean Thread Noodles

Rice Vermicelli

Noodles (*pancit*) *Pancit* is the general Filipino term for noodles. Noodles symbolize prosperity, long life, and good luck, making them a popular birthday fare. Filipinos believe the longer the noodles the better, so noodles are usually not cut when cooked. There is a wide range of noodles, and each type has a different texture and taste. Always follow the package instructions when cooking noodles.

Cornstarch Noodles (*luglug*) Often labeled *pancit luglug*, these round, thick, white-colored noodles are sold dried. After being cooked, they should be drained under running water to wash away excess starch. If the noodles are not rinsed after cooking, they will stick together.

Mung Bean Thread Noodles (*sotanghon*) These dried and white-colored noodles go by several names: "cellophane noodles," "Chinese vermicelli," "glass noodles." Mung bean thread noodles need to be soaked in water before they are added to the pan. The noodles turn transparent when cooked. They can be stir-fried or cooked in soups (no need to soak them then).

Rice Vermicelli (*bihon*) Also known as "rice thread noodles," are thin, dried noodles that do not turn transparent when cooked. Rice vermicelli is first soaked in water to soften before being added to the pan.

Wheat Noodles are commonly available in four types:

Canton Noodles These dried, round noodles are yellow-colored—either from eggs, which they are often made with, or from the addition of yellow food coloring. *Canton* noodles may be quickly dunked in hot water to soften or added at the last minute to a pan, as these noodles cook easily, despite their thick girth. This noodle is a good choice for stir-fried dishes.

Mami Noodles are normally made of wheat flour and egg. They are thin, often dried, and yellow-colored. Try to avoid using the imitation mami noodles that use yellow food coloring rather than eggs to obtain their yellow coloring. One popular story tells of the origin of mami. A Chinese entrepreneur named Ma Mon Luk promoted his noodle soup by calling out "Mami!" ("Ma" is his name and *mi* or *mee* is Chinese for noodles). Hence, mami has come to be associated with any type of hot noodle soup.

Miki Noodles are thick, wide and normally flat noodles that are yellow colored. They are a perfect noodle for soups. They are sometimes also called "Shanghai noodles."

Misua, also spelled *mee sua* or *miswa*, is a dried, thin, white-colored noodle with a silky smooth texture. They cook quickly and are a good choice for soups. They are also known as "angel hair pancit" or "Chinese vermicelli."

in height and the fruit can weigh up to 80 pounds (32 kg). Unripe jackfruits are cooked as a vegetable in some countries but ripe jackfruits are very popular in the Philippines as an ingredient in desserts. Green and prickly on the outside, the bright yellow fruit inside is soft and sweet and encases many hard, black seeds. You can normally buy the fruit already peeled, which is better because it is messy and time-consuming to peel it yourself. Look in Asian, Latin American, and Middle Eastern grocery stores. Frozen, bottled, and canned jackfruits are also widely available. Other sweet fuits like pear and mango may be used in place of jackfruit.

Long Beans (*sitaw*) are also known as "yardlong beans," "snake beans" or "runner beans" and can grow to about 18 inches (45 cm). Like green beans, they are typically sliced and sautèed or boiled, although they are not as juicy as green beans. They don't store well, so use them within a few days of purchase. Green beans make a good substitute.

Miso Paste (*miso*) is made from fermented ground soybeans and is used for sauces and soups. Miso comes in brown, white, or black. Look for it in Asian or health food stores. Use fermented black beans or bean paste if you cannot find miso.

Mung Beans (*monggo*) are tiny green beans that are best known as the basis for common bean sprouts. Sweetened and dried mung bean paste is used for cakes and snacks while mung bean starch is used to make mung bean thread noodles. Dried mung beans are available in Asian or Indian grocery stores.

Purple Yam (*ube*) Powder The purple yam, or *ube*, is very different from regular yams. This root crop is bigger, has a darker, rougher-looking skin, and a distinct purple flesh. Its dried and ground purple yam powder is used in a wide variety of desserts either for flavoring or color. It is sold in plastic packages in Asian grocery stores or online stores. Frozen ube and bottled ready-made ube pastes are available too.

Rice Flour is milled rice that is usually sold in packets or boxes in Asian grocery stores. Rice flour can be made into *galapong*, or rice balls, and is also called *mochiko*. It can be used to thicken sauces. You can also substitute all-purpose flour but the texture will be different. Glutinous rice flour, on the other hand, is normally used for desserts and steamed snacks.

Sautéed Shrimp Paste, or *bagoong alamang*, is a salty fermented paste made from baby shrimp. *Bagoong* means "fermented" in Filipino. This popular ingredient has a strong, pungent smell and varies in appearance, color, and flavor. *Ginisang bagoong* refers to ready-to-eat sautéed fermented shrimp paste sold in jars in Philippine supermarkets and Asian grocery stores. Filipinos love to spoon the bagoong over vegetable and meat dishes, even on food that may already be well seasoned. Bottled bagoong products are sold in Asian stores, look for those imported from the Philippines. The Indonesian *terasi*, Malaysian

belachan, Thai *kapi*, and Vietnamese *mam tom* are good substitutes.

Spring Roll Wrappers (Fresh) The round, white-yellowish, crepelike, wafer-thin wrappers are about about 8 inches (20 cm) and usually frozen. They are made of wheat flour, water, coconut oil, salt, and eggs (sometimes without eggs). They are also called "pastry wrappers," "lumpia wrappers" or "lumpia skins" (*balat ng lumpia*). Look for the packet that has a picture of fresh spring rolls. Before using, thaw the wrappers fully. Leftover wrappers should be stored in a tightly sealed plastic bag before putting them back into the freezer; otherwise, they will become dry and unusable. Dried rice paper wrappers used to wrap Vietnamese spring rolls and usually found in the dried noodle section, are not advisable for the Filipino fresh spring roll version.

Spring Roll Wrappers (Fried) These are square wrappers and are slightly thicker than the fresh spring roll ones. They are also labeled "spring roll pastry" and are available frozen. They are made from wheat flour, water, coconut oil, and salt and sometimes eggs. The sizes vary, so cut the large ones before serving. Thaw the wrappers completely before using. If you wish to store the leftover wrappers, place them in a tightly sealed plastic bag. Look for the packet that has a picture of deep-fried spring rolls. Either the Filipino or Chinese spring roll wrappers may be used.

Tamarind (*sampalok*) fruit ripe tamarind is sweet and is great for jams and candies, unripe tamarind is great for sour *sinigang* soups. The inside is green and very sour. To make the base for sinigang, the shelled tamarind is boiled, mashed, strained, and mixed with the soup. Frozen tamarind fruits and ready-to-use tamarind paste are sold in bags. If not available, look for the tamarind *sinigang* concentrate in powder or cubes in Asian grocery stores.

Tapioca Pearls are made from the cassava plant. They have a similar appearance and taste as sago pearls, which are made from the piths of sago palms that are widely grown in the Southern Philippines. To cook the dried pearls, bring to a boil four parts of water and one part of uncooked pearls. Add brown sugar (according to desired sweetness) and simmer for 20 minutes. Dried tapioca pearls are sold in various sizes and colors. Dry sago is sold in packages, and cooked sago is in jars. They can be found in Asian and Latin American grocery stores.

Taro Root (*gabi*) is a traditional staple in many tropical countries. It has a brown, coarse skin and gray- or purple-tinged flesh with a nutty flavor. The size of taro roots varies, but the Filipino variety is about the size of an orange. Taro is prepared like a potato. Peeled, sliced and cooked, taro is a basic ingredient for *sinigang* soups as well as for desserts. Firm taro root will keep for about a week at room temperature. Look for them at Asian markets and natural foods store. Jerusalem artichokes, sometimes called "sunchoke," or potatoes may be substituted.

Toasted Rice (*pinipig*) is toasted, pounded glutinous rice. Upon harvest, the

still-green glutinous rice is pounded flat in a mortar and pestle, and then toasted. *Pinipig* smells great and is used as a topping for desserts or can be actually eaten like a cereal. Sold in a plastic packages, pinipig looks like crispy rice cereal (which can be a substitute for pinipig).

Tofu (*tokwa*) There are many varieties of tofu (bean curd). In the Philippines, soft tofu is rarely used and the most common form is the tokwa, which is pressed tofu, sold in cakes. Fried tokwa has a crisp, brown exterior but firm, white inside. Tokwa lasts longer—for about two weeks—than regular tofu when refrigerated. Look for it in the frozen section of Asian or vegetarian/health food stores. Deep-fried tofu, pressed tofu, or extra-firm tofu can be used in its place.

Water Chestnuts are root tubers that are similar to chestnuts in color and shape. When using, cut off the top, peel the skin using a vegetable peeler, and then slice them. The small and round root has a crispy white flesh that retains its crispiness even when cooked. The flavor is bland with a hint of sweetness. It is widely cultivated in paddy fields and marshes in the Philippines. Look for firm water chestnuts with unwrinkled skins. Unpeeled fresh water chestnuts can be stored up to three weeks in the refrigerator. Jicama is a good substitute, but canned water chestnuts are widely available.

Water Spinach (*kangkong*) also called "convolvulus," is a nutritious leafy green vegetable that grows in water—making it important to wash the greens thoroughly before cooking. The edible stems are hollow and the pointed leaves are long and thin. Try to use them as soon as they are bought because they do not keep well. Spinach can be used as a substitute.

Wonton Wrappers, or "wonton skins," are 4-inch (10-cm) squares made from wheat flour, water, eggs, and salt. The thickness varies depending on the brand. Choose thinner ones for use in wonton soup dumplings as the thicker wrappers are for frying. Once filled with ground meat, wonton wrappers can be easily folded and sealed. They have a soft and silky texture when boiled. They are found in the frozen section, next to the tofu or fresh noodles. There are also round dumpling wrappers in the frozen section but these don't have the same melt-in-the-mouth texture when cooked. Leftover wrappers should be stored in a tightly sealed plastic bag before putting them back into the freezer; otherwise, they will become dry and unusable.

Cooking Utensils and Techniques

One of the best features of Filipino food is that it is simple to prepare and does not require special skills or exotic cooking utensils. Even rather complicated-looking dishes, such as *tamales*, can be prepared in any kitchen.

On Filipino Cooking Techniques

Filipino dishes do not require elaborate preparations, special cooking methods or presentations. Cooking the Filipino way seems to be a natural extension of the lifestyle of everyday home cooks. Though modern short-cuts and conveniences are used in Filipino kitchens today, the simple roots of the cuisine are evident in the no-fuss recipes that comprise the cooking of the Philippines.

Early Filipinos boiled, steamed and roasted their food until Chinese migrants taught them the art of stir-frying and deep-frying and brought the indispensable soy sauce and other condiments to the wok and dining table. The next wave of innovation to Filipino cooking came when the Spanish colonizers brought with them chili peppers, tomatoes sauces, corn, potatoes and the method of sautéing. In the mid-twentieth century, Americans introduced convenience foods, such as canned meats and canned fruit cocktail, to the country, leading to new Filipino dishes using existing cooking techniques.

Herbs or spices do not feature heavily in Filipino cooking, though black peppercorns and bay leaves (or "laurel") are used. Instead, fish sauce and shrimp paste are the popular and common ways to add flavor to dishes, similar to the way Westerners use salt, pepper, or ketchup. Further, vinegar adds tang; *calamansi*, a bright, tart accent; and tamarind, a sour counterpoint.

Chef's Knife or Cleaver

A good cleaver is essential because Filipino dishes are mainly chopped into bitesize pieces prior to cooking. Also known as Chinese cleaver, it is a large, heavy knife with a square blade about 3 inches (7 cm) wide. It is useful for cutting through bones; mincing meat, fish, and vegetables; and crushing garlic cloves. Its wide blade is also useful for transporting chopped food from the cutting board into the pan.

Cutting Board

Most wooden cutting boards in the Philippines are made of narra. Good quality wooden boards can be passed down from generation to generation and have advantages over plastic ones. Wood possesses anti-microbial properties, shallow cuts will close up on their own. Wooden cutting boards don't dull knives but they are not dishwasher friendly, so choose a cutting board that fits your sink. You don't need to have several cutting boards but a small one can be very useful for quick tasks.

Mortar and Pestle

A mortar and pestle set can be found in every Filipino kitchen. This fundamental tool is used to crush garlic, peanuts, and other spices and to extract shrimp juice. It is also used to crush a little bit of chocolate, or break down any hard food into smaller pieces.

Saucepans and Skillets

The majority of Filipino cooking is done in saucepans (or pots) and skillets with lids. The most common sizes are a 9- or 10-inch (23 or 25-cm) skillet, a 1- to 2-quart (1 liter to 1.75-liter) saucepan, and a 4-quart (3.75-liter) saucepan.

Wok

Locally known as *kawali* or *talyasi* and made from cast iron, woks are amazingly versatile for stir-frying, deep-frying, steaming, and braising. The traditional woks with round bottoms can be used only on gas ranges, but they are useful for deep-frying as they require less oil than other cookware. You can find various types of woks including carbon steel ones. Non-stick woks coated with Teflon are popular but susceptible to scratches and are not suitable for cooking at high heat. Woks come in various sizes but a 12-inch (30-cm) wok will serve much of your cooking needs. If you are getting one, it is a good idea to make sure it will fit in your sink because traditional woks are not dishwasher friendly.

How to Deep-Fry

The trick to achieving properly deep-fried food with a crisp exterior and delicious (not greasy!) interior is heating the frying oil to the correct temperature of between 350 and 375°F (175 to 190°C) and maintaining that temperature when frying food in batches. Here are a few helpful tips:

• You can use a specially designed deep-fryer, but any deep pot that is roomy enough will do.

• Use an oil with a high-smoke point, such as canola, grape seed oil or corn oil. Do not use olive oil.

• Use enough oil to completely submerge the food (this amount will depend on the size of the food and the dimensions of the pot), but do not fill the deep-fryer or pot more than half-way full. The latter is important to avoid spillovers or splatters.

• Test the oil temperature before adding the food with either a deep-fryer thermometer or by inserting a wooden chopstick or skewer. (If it is hot enough, bubbles will form all around the stick.)

• If you have a large amount of food, deep-fry it in batches so as not to crowd the pan.

• Remove fried food with slotted spoon or a skimmer and drain in single layers on paper towels.

• To reuse the oil, allow it to cool, strain through a fine-mesh sieve lined with cheesecloth, and store in the refrigerator. If the oil develops a rancid or "off" smell, or if it smells like the foods you've deep-fried in it, discard it.

How to Stir-Fry

This method of fast, high-heat cooking is typically done in a wok, but a large skillet can also be used. The advantage of using a wok is that you can push the food that is already cooked to the cooler sloping sides of the wok, leaving the food that is not yet cooked in the center of the wok that is directly over the heat source. Here are some helpful tips for stir-frying with success:

• Prepare all the ingredients you plan to stir-fry before you begin cooking, and have all sauces or condiments at the ready. Once the stir-frying begins, the process goes very quickly, so it's important to have all prep work completed beforehand.

• For the best appearance, cut all ingredients to approximately the same size. If not all ingredients cook at the same rate, you will need to add them sequentially, starting with the longest cooking ingredients. On the other hand, if you don't mind that the ingredients are cut into different sizes, you may cut the longest-cooking ingredients into the smallest size and cut the quickest-cooking ingredients into the largest size. This will enable you to add all the vegetables and meat to the wok at the same time, space allowing.

• Heat the wok or skillet over high heat and then add oil. When the oil is hot, add any aromatics you may be using, such as ginger and garlic, and stir-fry for a few seconds, or until they become fragrant. Then quickly add another ingredient.

• Do not overcrowd the wok. If crowded, food will steam rather than stir-fry. If you have too much food for the size of the wok or skillet that you are using, stir-fry the food in batches, starting with the meat (after the aromatics, of course). Then remove the meat, add the vegetables, and return the meat just before the vegetables are done. Sauce or liquids (such as soy sauce) added for flavoring and seasoning are added near the end of cooking.

How to Make Annatto Water

Annatto seeds are little red seeds that, when mixed with warm water, produce a natural red food coloring. The red coloring is used in Filipino, Latin America, and Caribbean dishes. It has a bland taste with a hint of nutmeg. Annatto water is commonly used for the shrimp sauce in Noodles with Shrimp and Tofu (page 94) and the base for the Oxtail Vegetable Stew (page 56) as it gives these dishes an appetizing red-orange color. Use a spoon when extracting the color from the seeds or you'll end up with reddish fingers.

1 tablespoon annatto seeds
1/2 cup (125 ml) warm water

Place the seeds and warm water in a bowl, preferably a glass bowl. Let stand for 2 minutes or more. Press the seeds with the back of a spoon for about 5 minutes or until the water becomes reddish in color. Strain the liquid and reserve. Discard the seeds.

How to Crush Garlic

Many Filipino recipes call for garlic to be crushed whether it is used whole or then chopped or minced. Crushing garlic before chopping or mincing it releases more flavor and aroma, and it's a very expedient way to peel it as well. I prefer to use a mortar and pestle when crushing several cloves of garlic at once.

Using a knife:
1. Place a garlic clove on a chopping board.
2. Place the wide side of the knife on top of the clove and whack the area that is directly over the cloves with your fist (the side opposite the thumb), smashing the garlic.
3. The skin should come off easily. Discard the skin, and then chop, if necessary.

Using a mortar and pestle:
1. Place the cloves of unpeeled garlic in the middle of the mortar. An average mortar will comfortably hold 3 to 5 cloves. Crush the cloves by smashing them with the pestle. It takes some practice to not make the cloves jump out from the hollow of the mortar.
2. The skin should come off easily. Discard the skin, and then chop, if necessary.

Basic Recipes

A Filipino meal is often accompanied with several *sawsawan*, or dipping sauces. Filipinos like to adjust and intensify the flavors of their food to fit their personal taste. They do this with a little bit of soy sauce, fish sauce, shrimp paste, vinegar, hot peppers or garlic. In this section are popular Filipino sauces that are usually drizzled over meats or used as dips and condiments, such as Liver Paste (page 23), Crispy Fried Garlic (page 23), Tomato and Salted Egg Salad (page 22) and Pickled Green Papaya (page 21), that are mixed with rice. It's worthwhile learning how to make them because they go along with any fried food. The centerpiece of every Filipino meal is steamed rice, so the easy and foolproof Filipino way to cook steamed rice on stovetop is also included.

Garlic Mayonnaise Dip

This all-purpose dipping sauce goes well with Crispy Fried Fishballs (page 33) or Crunchy Fried Squid (page 27). It keeps for a week if stored in an airtight container in the refrigerator.

Makes about 1/2 cup (75 g)
Preparation time: 5 minutes

1/2 cup (125 ml) mayonnaise
3 cloves garlic, crushed with the side of a
    knife and minced
1/2 teaspoon salt
1/4 teaspoon freshly ground black pepper

Combine all ingredients in a small bowl, and mix thoroughly.

Vinegar Garlic Sauce

Simple yet essential, this sauce goes well with Fried Marinated Fish (page 74), Filipino Fried Chicken (page 65) and Roasted Marinated Pork (page 46). Keep in an airtight container and use the dip within a week.

Makes about 1/2 cup (125 ml)
Preparation time: 5 minutes

1/2 cup (125 ml) Filipino cane vinegar (or
    white vinegar or cider vinegar diluted with
    water, page 13)
3 cloves garlic, crushed with the side of a
    knife and minced
1 teaspoon pepper

Combine all ingredients in a small bowl, and mix thoroughly.

Garlic Mayonnaise Dip

Pickled Green Papaya

Sweet and Spicy Sauce

Vinegar Garlic Sauce

Tomato and Salted Egg Salad

Sweet and Spicy Sauce

This sauce is perfect for seafood. Serve with Crispy Fried Fishballs (page 33), Stuffed Crabs (page 76) or Fried Shrimp with Assorted Dips (page 26). If stored in an airtight container in the refrigerator, it can keep up to a week.

Makes about 1/3 cup (80 ml)
Preparation time: 5 minutes

1 tablespoon olive oil
4 tablespoons banana ketchup or tomato ketchup
1 tablespoon sugar
1 finger-length green chili pepper, deseeded and minced

Combine all ingredients in a small bowl, and mix thoroughly.

Pickled Green Papaya
Achara

This Indian-influenced side dish— achar means "pickle" in many Indian languages—is a delicious accompaniment to anything, and is a regular item on every Filipino table. It goes particularly well with Fried Marinated Fish (page 74) or Barbequed Chicken Skewers (page 61). It keeps well for a couple of months in the refrigerator.

Makes about 3 cups (450 g)
Preparation time: 15 minutes
Cooking time: 20 minutes

3 cloves garlic, minced or crushed
One 2-inch (5-cm) piece fresh ginger, peeled and thinly sliced
1 cup (250 ml) Filipino cane vinegar (or white vinegar or cider vinegar diluted with water, page 13)
4 tablespoons sugar
1 tablespoon salt
1 unripe papaya (1 1/3 lbs/600 g), peeled, deseeded, and grated to yield 2 cups (400 g) grated papaya
1 carrot, peeled and grated

1/2 cup (50 g) raisins
1 cup (100 g) chopped pineapple
1 fresh bell pepper, deseeded and thinly sliced
1 teaspoon freshly ground black pepper

Combine the garlic, ginger, vinegar, sugar, and salt in a saucepan, and bring to a boil. Cook over medium-high heat, uncovered, for 5 minutes.

Add the rest of the ingredients. Cover and cook over medium-low heat for 15 minutes. Set aside to cool.

Transfer to a jar with a tight lid. Store in the refrigerator.

Vinegar and Sautéed Shrimp Paste Sauce

This sauce can be served as a dressing for Filipino Spinach Salad (page 85) or as a dipping sauce for Fried Marinated Fish (page 74). Consume the sauce the same day.

Makes about 1/3 cup (80 ml)
Preparation time: 5 minutes

3 tablespoons Filipino cane vinegar (or white vinegar or cider vinegar diluted with water, page 13)
1 clove garlic, crushed with the side of a knife and minced
1/2 teaspoon sugar
1/2 teaspoon freshly ground black pepper
1 tablespoon fish sauce
1 1/4 teaspoons bottled sautéed shrimp paste (page 16)
1 tablespoon freshly squeezed lime juice

Combine all ingredients in a small bowl, and mix thoroughly.

Sweet Garlic Sauce

Dip the Fresh Pork Salad Rolls (page 32) or the Crispy Fried Fishballs (page 33) in this sauce. Store in an airtight container in the refrigerator and it keeps for a week.

Makes about 1 cup (250 ml)
Preparation time: 10 minutes
Cooking time: 5 minutes

3 cloves garlic, crushed with the side of a knife and minced
3 tablespoons brown sugar
1 teaspoon salt
2 tablespoons soy sauce
1 tablespoon Filipino cane vinegar (or white vinegar or cider vinegar diluted with water, page 13)
1 cup (250 ml) water
1 tablespoon cornstarch dissolved in 2 tablespoons of water

Combine the garlic, sugar, salt, soy sauce, vinegar, and water in a saucepan, and bring to a boil. Reduce the heat to low and add the cornstarch mixture. Stir until thickened, and remove from the heat.

Sweet and Sour Sauce

This versatile sauce may be served with Crispy Fried Fishballs (page 33), Spring Rolls (page 31), Fried Shrimp with Assorted Dips (page 26) or Crunchy Fried Squid (page 27). It can be stored in an airtight container in the refrigerator for about a week.

Makes about 1 cup (250 ml)
Preparation time: 10 minutes

1 teaspoon sugar
1 cup (250 ml) Filipino cane vinegar (or white vinegar or cider vinegar diluted with water, page 13)
2 cloves garlic, crushed with the side of a knife and minced
1 finger-length red chili pepper, minced
1 teaspoon cornstarch dissolved in 1 tablespoon of water
1 teaspoon salt
1 tablespoon ketchup

Combine all ingredients in a small bowl, and mix thoroughly.

Spicy Garlic Vinegar Dipping Sauce

This flavorful sauce is typically served with Papaya Shrimp Fritters (page 33), Spring Rolls (page 31), Crunchy Fried Squid (page 27), Fried Shrimp with Assorted Dips (page 26) or Roasted Marinated Pork (page 46). It is best to consume the sauce the same day.

Makes about 1/2 cup (125 ml)
Preparation time: 5 minutes

1/2 cup (125 ml) Filipino cane vinegar (or white vinegar or cider vinegar diluted with water, page 13)
1/4 teaspoon freshly ground black pepper
5 cloves garlic, crushed with the side of a knife and minced
1 finger-length green chili pepper, deseeded and minced

Combine all ingredients in a small bowl, and mix thoroughly.

Tomato and Salted Egg Salad

Salty eggs, juicy ripe tomatoes, and tart lime juice can be a refreshing combination. You can also add lettuce, chopped green onion, and marinated olives to augment the combination.

Serves 4
Preparation time: 5 minutes

3 hard-boiled Salted Eggs (see recipe, right), shelled and diced
2 ripe tomatoes, diced
1/4 teaspoon freshly ground black pepper
1 tablespoon freshly squeezed calamansi juice (or lime juice)

Combine the egg, tomato, pepper, and lime juice in a mixing bowl. Mix thoroughly.

Salted Eggs

Salted Eggs
Itlog na Maalat

Salted egg, known as *itlog na maalat*, is a common fixture on every Filipino table. In tropical countries like the Philippines, this is one way to preserve eggs. Salted eggs are often dyed a deep red to distinguish them from fresh eggs. Filipinos love to combine chopped salted eggs with tomatoes (see Tomato and Salted Egg Salad on this page) or have them with Fried Marinated Fish (page 74) or Roasted Marinated Pork (page 46). Salted eggs are also used to garnish pastries and as a topping or filler for steamed buns (*siopao*). Because of their bigger, richer yolks and thicker shells, duck eggs are traditionally used but chicken eggs work fine too. To make salted eggs, eggs are soaked for about three weeks or more in a brine solution and keep them in a dark and dry place—preferably your cupboard. The eggs do not cure as quickly at cooler temperatures and the length of the curing period depends on the temperature. In the Philippines, the eggs cure after three weeks—but may take longer if you live in a cooler climate.

Preparation time: Minimum 3 weeks curing period
Cooking time: 30 minutes

8 fresh duck or chicken eggs
4 cups (1 liter) water
1 1/2 cups (300 g) salt

Place the eggs in a wide-mouthed jar with a lid.

Add the water to a saucepan and bring to a boil. Add the salt gradually. Stir until the salt is totally dissolved. Set aside to cool.

Pour the cooled saltwater over the eggs. The eggs should be completely submerged. Add more of the brine solution if needed.

Cover and store the jar in a dark place for at least 3 weeks. To test the egg's saltiness, take out one egg after 3 weeks, and boil it over high heat for 30 minutes (salted eggs take more time to cook than regular eggs). Let cool for a few minutes. Peel the shell and taste. If the saltiness is to your liking, take out the other eggs, boil, and store in the refrigerator. If you want a "saltier" salted egg, leave the eggs for another 2 weeks.

Crispy Fried Garlic

Fried garlic is a popular topping in Filipino cuisine, typically sprinkled on Rice Porridge with Chicken (page 92). It is also a perfect topping for pasta or salads. If you go to an Asian store, you can find precooked bottles or packets of fried garlic, but it's easy to make your own at home. You can store fried garlic in an airtight container or bottle for a couple of months without refrigeration.

Makes about 1/3 cup (70 g)
Preparation time: 5 minutes
Cooking time: 10 minutes

1/2 cup (125 ml) oil
10 cloves garlic, crushed with the side of a knife and minced

Add the oil to a skillet or wok and set over high heat. When hot, add the garlic and stir-ly until brown and crispy. Perfectly fried garlic should be crisp and golden brown on the outside and be slightly moist on the inside. Be careful not to burn the garlic (quickly remove the pan from the heat once it begins to brown). Strain the garlic and place on a paper towel to absorb the excess oil.

Liver Paste

This rich paste adds flavor to stews (I use it on Kaldereta Beef Stew, page 53) and is also the base for the popular Filipino sauce called Lechon Sauce that is served with Crispy Lechon Pork (page 48). It keeps refrigerated for a couple of days. Ready-made canned versions of liver paste are widely available in supermarkets.

Makes about 1 cup (200 g)
Preparation time: 5 minutes
Cooking time: 30 minutes

4 cups (1 liter) plus 3 tablespoons water
1/2 lb (250 g) liver (chicken, pork or beef), sliced
1 tablespoon salt
1 small onion, chopped

Pour the 4 cups (1 liter) of water into a saucepan and bring to a boil. Add the liver and salt and cook over high heat for 20 minutes. Drain and set aside to cool. Roughly chop the liver.

Place the chopped liver, the onion and the 3 remaining tablespoons of water into a food processor or blender. Blend until the mixture becomes spreadable. If it is too thick, add a little more water.

Perfect Steamed Rice

Non-Filipinos often find Filipino food a bit salty. (If you live in the tropics, you always perspire and your body craves for salt!) The neutralizer for this "saltiness" is steamed rice. Two parts steamed rice and one part main dish (or "viand") is usually the correct combination to strike a balance.

Most Filipinos say that steamed rice is the main dish and that the goodness of the meal depends on the goodness of the steamed rice. A general rule of thumb is that one person consumes about three cups of steamed rice per meal—and one cup of uncooked rice makes three cups of cooked rice.

Today, many people use rice cookers but in the rural areas of the Philippines, it is still common to cook rice using a *kaldero*, a special pot made of cast iron specifically designed to cook rice on the stovetop. It is thick enough to avoid the rice being burnt.

Cooking perfect steamed rice on the stovetop takes a little practice. To create fluffy rice, one needs to use the right amount of water, the right level of heat, a heavy-bottomed pot, and a tight lid to trap the steam (steam finishes the cooking during the "resting" period).

Different types of rice need different amounts of water. As a general rule though, the ratio of water to long-grain white rice should be a bit less than double. You may need to experiment to find out the best ratio for the specific rice you are using. New crop rice, or rice harvested in the same year that it is sold, is not as

dry as old rice so it needs slightly less water. In general, too much water results in softer and stickier rice (and may even resemble porridge), less water results in hard (sometimes uncooked) steamed rice. The best way to produce perfectly steamed rice is to use the same kind and brand of rice and the same saucepan, and experiment until you get it right.

Serves 4 to 6
Cooking time: 25 minutes

4 cups (800 g) white long-grain rice (jasmine rice)
Approximately 7 cups (1.75 liters) water

Place the rice in a heavy-bottomed saucepan, cover with water and wash the rice thoroughly in order to remove the excess starch. (Some mills use talc powder as a milling aid, so it's important to rinse the rice thoroughly.) Swish the rice around with your fingers and discard the milky water (or use it to make Fish Soup with Miso Dip, page 36) without pouring any rice out of the saucepan. Add water again and wash the rice 2 more times, or until the water runs clear. Drain well.

Add the water to the pan and level the rice by rocking the pan so the rice settles evenly at the bottom. Measure the level of the water by lowering your hand—palm open and fingers stretched down, and touching the bottom of the pan—and noting where the level of the rice is against the level of the water. The level of the water should be almost twice as high as the level of the rice.

Place the saucepan over high heat and bring to a boil. When the rice starts bubbling, turn the heat down to the lowest setting, cover with a tight-fitting lid, and leave for about 20 minutes. Do not lift the lid while cooking as this will interrupt the steaming process.

Turn off the heat and let stand for another 20 minutes with the lid still on. (Leave for another 10 more minutes or longer if cooking more than 4 cups of rice.) The steam inside the pot will finish the cooking. When cooked, transfer the rice to a serving bowl and place on the middle of the table. Serve hot.

chapter 1
appetizers
and snacks

Although there is a word in Tagalog for appetizers (*pampagana*), a more accurate translation would be "small bite." In the Philippines, appetizers are not served separately during mealtime. Rather, all of the prepared dishes, including fruits and some desserts, are placed on the table at the same time, including fruits and some desserts, buffet style. There are no rules as to what food should be eaten first; you can have a bite of your favorite banana fritters before eating your vegetables!

One of the Spanish habits that the Filipinos adopted as their own is enjoying snacks at various times of the day, called *merienda*. In the Philippines, it is not uncommon to have two meriendas in a day, where everyone enjoys a simple snack between meals to help them refuel until the next large meal. Ubiquitous street vendors and roadside stalls offer various delicacies—fishballs, rice cakes, spring rolls and all sorts of *palamig* (coolers) to hungry and thirsty clients. Merienda may seem like just another excuse to snack all day long, but it's an integral part of Filipino culture. In a sweltering country like the Philippines, you'll look for a regular break from whatever you are doing for that tall glass of refreshing mango juice or some delicious tamales at a reasonable price. Besides being an excuse to eat, merienda is also another way to bond with the family and friends and to socialize and gossip.

Many of the recipes in this section, such as Fresh Pork Salad Rolls (page 32), Spring Rolls (page 31), and Fried Shrimp with Assorted Dips (page 26), are popular finger foods (*pica pica*) that are also meals in themselves, especially when served with hot steamed rice. Feel free to serve any of these dishes as a first course, a party snack, or along with several other dishes as a main course.

Fried Shrimp with Assorted Dips

Camaron Rebosado

In this dish, fresh shrimp are dunked in batter, deep-fried to golden perfection, and typically served with Sweet and Sour Sauce. This is one of several Filipino staples with Spanish names that are actually Chinese in origin. Many Chinese immigrants came to the Philippines and settled here. When the Spanish arrived, Chinese eateries were already flourishing and Chinese dishes were soon given Spanish names.

Serves 4 to 6
Preparation time: 15 minutes
Cooking time: 30 minutes

3 tablespoons all-purpose flour
1 teaspoon salt
1 teaspoon baking powder
1/2 cup (125 ml) water
1 egg, beaten
2 cups (500 ml) oil for deep-frying (page 18)
1 lb (500 g) fresh shrimp, shelled and deveined (leave the tails on)
Sweet and Sour Sauce (page 21), Sweet and Spicy Sauce (page 21), or Garlic Mayonnaise Dip (page 20), for dipping

Combine the flour, salt, baking powder, and water in a mixing bowl. Mix thoroughly until smooth. Add the egg into the mixture and stir well.

Heat a small saucepan or wok over high heat and add the oil. Use a wooden chopstick or skewer to check if the oil is hot enough. When it's hot enough, bubbles will form all around the stick. (Or use a deep-fryer thermometer to read the temperature, which should be between 350° and 375°F or 175° and 190°C when ready.) Reduce the heat to medium once it reaches the desired temperature so that the oil doesn't burn.

Holding a shrimp by its tail, dip it in the flour mixture and gently drop it directly into the oil. Repeat the process with the rest of the shrimp, dropping the shrimp into the oil one by one. Deep-fry the shrimp until lightly browned. Do not overcrowd the pan. Drain on paper towels. Serve with Sweet and Sour Sauce, Sweet and Spicy Sauce or Garlic Mayonnaise Dip.

Fried Shrimp with Assorted Dips (left) and Crunchy Fried Squid (right).

Crunchy Fried Squid

Calamares

This is everybody's favorite *pulutan,* or finger food, which goes especially well with cold beer or wine. Calamares are one of the quickest and easiest Filipino seafood dishes to prepare. I usually cook this dish for parties. Simply squeeze lemon juice over the fried squid and then dip them in any of the dips listed in the recipe. Frozen squid can be used, but fresh squid tastes better.

Serves 4 to 6
Preparation time: 10 minutes
Cooking time: 20 minutes

1 lb (500 g) medium-sized fresh squid or pre-cleaned frozen squid (instructions on how to clean fresh squid on page 70)
1 teaspoon salt
1/2 cup (60 g) flour
1 egg, beaten
2 cups (500 ml) oil for deep-frying (page 18)
Sweet and Sour Sauce (page 21), Spicy Garlic Vinegar Dipping Sauce (page 22), Garlic Mayonnaise Dip (page 20) or banana ketchup, for dipping

Clean the squid and cut them into rings (you may include the head). Pat dry with paper towels. Mix the salt and flour thoroughly in the mixing bowl. Dredge each ring in the egg then coat it with the flour mixture.

Heat a medium saucepan or wok over high heat and add the oil. Use a wooden chopstick or skewer to check if the oil is hot enough. When it's hot enough, bubbles will form all around the stick. (Or use a deep-fryer thermometer to read the temperature, which should be between 350° and 375°F or 175° and 190°C when ready.) Reduce the heat to medium once it reaches the desired temperature so that the oil doesn't burn.

Deep-fry the squid for about 7 minutes or until lightly browned. Do not overcrowd the pan. Drain on paper towels. If you fry the squid for too long, they become tough. Transfer to a serving platter. Serve immediately with Sweet and Sour Sauce, Spicy Garlic Vinegar Dipping Sauce, Garlic Mayonnaise Dip or banana ketchup.

Chicken Tamales

Tamales, or *tamal* in *Spanish*, are a traditional Mexican snack, made with steam-cooked corn filling wrapped in cornhusks, that the Spanish introduced to the Philippines. The Filipinos modified the dish by using a mixture of finely ground rice, chicken, egg, that is then wrapped in banana leaves instead of cornhusks. Once boiled, the tamale is unwrapped and the sweet rice filling is spooned out and eaten. The cooked ground rice turns jellylike and has the sweet, subtle aroma of banana leaves. Although the process of making tamales is simple, it does take some practice to perfect the wrapping part. It's important to double-wrap the filling and secure it properly so that it does not open during boiling.

Heat a skillet over high heat and add the uncooked rice. Lower the heat to medium and toast the rice until lightly browned, stirring constantly. Remove the rice and pound with a mortar and pestle, or use a food processor to grind it into a fine powder. If using rice flour, toast in the skillet until lightly browned. Set aside.

In a saucepan, simmer the ground rice, 2 cups (500 ml) of water, coconut milk, sugar, salt and pepper over low heat until the mixture thickens, stirring regularly.

Heat the chicken and annatto water in a separate saucepan over medium heat, stirring constantly for 5 minutes, or until the chicken becomes orange. Drain and set aside.

Cut each banana leaf into 10-inch (25-cm) squares. Soften each banana leaf square over an open flame or scald it for about 5 seconds with boiling water, then drain. The leaf will soften and makes wrapping easier.

Place a banana leaf, lighter side up, on a clean surface and place about 1 1/2 tablespoons of the rice mixture, a piece of chicken, 3 peanuts, and a slice of egg on top.

Fold the left and right sides of the leaf over the mixture, then fold the bottom and top of the leaf to form a square. Place the wrapped mixture in the center of another banana square. Fold it in the same way and tie it with kitchen twine. If using foil, wrap the mixture first in parchment paper and then in aluminum foil.

Pour the 10 cups (2.5 liters) of water into a stockpot and bring to a boil. Drop the tamales into the boiling water and cook over high heat for 30 minutes. Remove the tamales with a slotted spoon and let cool to room temperature.

Yields about 10 tamales
Preparation time: 30 minutes
Cooking time: 45 minutes

2 cups (400 g) uncooked long grain rice (or rice flour)
2 cups (500 ml) water
One 13 1/2-oz (400-ml) can coconut milk
1 teaspoon brown sugar
1 teaspoon table salt
1/4 teaspoon freshly ground black pepper
1 boneless, skinless chicken breast, cooked and sliced
1/2 cup (125 ml) annatto water (page 19)
10 sheets 10-in (25-cm) squares banana leaves
1/4 cup (50 g) roasted peanuts
2 hard-boiled eggs, thinly sliced
Kitchen twine, for tying the tamales squares
10 cups (2.5 liters) water

Chicken Empanadas

Empanadas (meaning "wrapped in bread") are found around the world. These half-moon pastries are typically filled with potato, chicken, onion, and raisins, but each of Spain's colonies have created their own version. Ground pork or beef may be substituted for the chicken.

To make the Dough, mix the flour, baking powder, butter, salt, and sugar in a mixing bowl and mix thoroughly. Add the water, 1 tablespoon at a time, until the dough can be gathered into a ball. Wrap it in plastic wrap and store in the refrigerator for 1 hour. While the dough is chilling, make the Filling.

To make the Filling, pour the water into a saucepan and bring to a boil. Add the chicken and boil for about 10 minutes, or until done (the flesh should appear opaque). Remove the chicken from the water with a slotted spoon, and set aside.

Boil the potatoes in a separate saucepan for 10 minutes or until done. Remove and drain the potatoes, then mash them in a bowl and add the thinly sliced cooked chicken.

Heat a skillet over medium heat and add the oil. When hot, add the garlic and sauté until lightly browned. Add the onion and sauté until translucent. Add the bacon and sauté for about 5 minutes or until lightly browned. Add the sautéed bacon, garlic, and onion as well as the raisins, butter, parsley, salt and pepper to the potato and chicken mixture. Mix thoroughly and set aside to cool completely. (It's important to let the filling cool off before making the pastries or the crust will get soggy.)

Preheat the oven to 375°F (190°C). Remove the chilled dough from the refrigerator. Take a piece of dough about the size of a golf ball (about 1-inch/2.5-cm in diameter) and, on a floured surface, flatten it with a rolling pin into a 1/8-inch (3-mm)-thick disk.

Place about 1 tablespoon of the Filling in the center of the disk. Fold the Dough over the Filling to form a half-moon shape. Press and seal the edges by running the prongs of the fork over the edges. Continue forming the Empanadas with the rest of the Dough and Filling.

Place the Empanadas on a lightly greased baking sheet. Brush the top of Empanadas with the egg and bake for about 30 minutes or until lightly browned.

Makes 15 empanadas
Preparation time: 30 minutes +
    1 hour to chill dough
Cooking time: 30 minutes

Filling
3 cups (750 ml) water
1 boneless, skinless chicken thigh, thinly sliced
2 potatoes, peeled and diced
1 tablespoon oil
3 cloves garlic, crushed with the side of knife and minced
1 onion, minced
3 strips bacon, thinly sliced
1/2 cup (100 g) raisins
1/2 cup (100 g) butter, melted
1 bunch fresh parsley, minced
1/2 teaspoon salt
1/4 teaspoon freshly ground black pepper
1 egg, beaten

Dough
3 cups (375 g) all-purpose flour
1 teaspoon baking powder
2 tablespoons butter, melted
1/2 teaspoon salt
2 tablespoons sugar
1/2 cup (125 ml) water

Pan de Sal Bread Rolls

Despite its name (*Pan de Sal* literally means "salt bread"), Pan de Sal Bread Rolls actually taste more sweet than salty. Originally made with just yeast, flour, water, and salt, the recipe has been improved over the years by adding sugar and breadcrumbs. Baking bread from scratch may seem a little daunting at first, but these rolls are very quick and easy to make (plus the smell of freshly baked bread in your kitchen makes it all worthwhile). These rolls are especially delicious when served with butter, or you can use them for making sandwiches—something that Filipinos love to do! I like eating them with Sweet Purple Yam Pudding (page 99) or Chicken Adobo (page 64).

Makes about 15 to 20 bread rolls
Preparation time: 20 minutes +
**   3 hours rising time**
Baking time: 20 minutes

1/2 cup (125 ml) lukewarm water
1/4 oz (1 envelope) active dry yeast
1 teaspoon plus 1/2 cup (100 g) sugar
1 cup (250 ml) water
3 tablespoons oil
1 tablespoon salt
5 cups (625 g) all-purpose flour
3 tablespoons breadcrumbs

Pour the lukewarm water (about 110° F/45°C) in a large mixing bowl, and add the yeast. Add 1 teaspoon of the sugar to activate the yeast, and stir gently to dissolve. Let stand in a warm place for 15 minutes.

Add the water, oil, 1/2 cup (100 g) of sugar, salt, and flour little by little and mix thoroughly. Knead the dough on a floured surface until smooth and pliable.

Place the kneaded dough in a large, lightly greased bowl. Cover with a clean kitchen cloth or hand towel and let rest in a warm place for 2 hours or until dough doubles in size. The ideal room temperature for bread dough to rise is about 75°F (24°C).

When the dough has doubled in size, place it on a floured surface. Punch the dough down and then divide it into 15 to 20 pieces. Form each roll into a ball with your hands.

Place the balls on a lightly greased baking sheet and sprinkle the breadcrumbs on top. Make sure to leave a little space between the rolls. Let them stand in a warm place for 1 hour or until they double in size.

Bake the rolls for about 20 minutes in a pre-heated oven (325°F or 160°C), or until lightly browned. To test if they are done, gently press the top of one of the rolls; if it springs back, it is done.

> ## Tips for baking bread:
> - Each oven bakes differently, so take time to get to know your oven. For instance, electric ovens tend to get hotter and cook faster than gas ovens.
> - Sometimes it is difficult to find a warm place to let the yeast or dough rise. Try putting it inside a preheated oven set to the lowest setting (and turn the oven off halfway through the rising process to make sure it doesn't cook the dough).
> - When dissolving the yeast in the lukewarm water, the temperature should be about 110°F (45°C). If the water is too hot or too cold, the dough will not rise.
> - Make sure to use fresh yeast. The dough will not rise properly if the yeast is expired.
> - It is tempting to add too much flour when kneading, but that will result in stiff bread.
> - Overbaked bread will turn hard after some time even if it looks fine right out of the oven.

Spring Rolls Lumpiang Shanghai

Serves 5
Preparation time: 20 minutes
Cooking time: 1 hour

Spring rolls are a great finger food that everybody loves. Filipinos know them as *lumpia*, which is derived from the Hokkien word meaning "mixed vegetables and meat rolled up." This version, Lumpiang Shanghai, refers to a spring roll stuffed with ground pork and then fried, but ground chicken, shrimp or crab can also be used. I always make some extra spring rolls and store them in the freezer for a quick meal later (frozen spring rolls don't need to be defrosted before deep-frying them). When frying, use medium heat to be sure that they cook through completely but be careful not to burn the outside. Use smaller 6-inch (15-cm)-square wrappers make perfect-sized rolls; if you use larger wrappers, simply cut the cooked spring rolls in half before serving.

Combine all the Filling ingredients in a bowl and mix thoroughly.

Place a wrapper on a flat surface and spread about a tablespoon of the Filling all along the bottom third of the wrapper. Roll the wrapper over the Filling, tuck in both ends, and roll it up tight. Moisten the edges of the wrapper with the egg white and press to seal.

Heat a medium saucepan or wok over high heat and add the oil. Use a wooden chopstick or skewer to check if the oil is hot enough. When it's hot enough, bubbles will form all around the stick. (Or use a deep-fryer thermometer to read the temperature, which should be between 350° and 375°F or 175° and 190°C when ready). Reduce the heat to medium once it reaches the desired temperature so that the oil doesn't burn.

Deep-fry until brown and crispy. Do not overcrowd the pan. Serve hot with Sweet and Sour Sauce or Spicy Garlic Vinegar Dipping Sauce. For a light meal, serve with hot steamed rice.

One 8.8-oz (250-g) package spring roll wrappers

1 egg white

2 cups (500 ml) oil for deep-frying (page 18)

Sweet and Sour Sauce (page 21) or Spicy Garlic Vinegar Dipping Sauce (page 22), for dipping

Filling

$1/_2$ lb (250 g) ground pork

2 water chestnuts, minced

1 medium onion, minced

1 small carrot, peeled and minced or grated

1 egg yolk

2 tablespoons soy sauce

3 cloves garlic, crushed with the side of knife and minced

$1/_4$ tablespoon salt

1 teaspoon freshly ground black pepper

Fresh Pork Salad Rolls

Lumpiang Sariwa

This variety of lumpia is the Filipino version of Chinese salad rolls. Unlike Lumpiang Shanghai, these rolls are not deep-fried. Instead, the filling rests on a lettuce leaf inside a spring roll wrapper. These spring rolls can make a substantial snack on their own but most Filipinos prefer to eat them with rice.

Make the Sweet Garlic Sauce, following the recipe on page 21.

Add 1 tablespoon of oil to a skillet over medium heat. When hot, add the garlic and sauté until lightly browned. Add the onion and sauté until translucent. Add the pork and sauté for about 5 minutes, or until cooked (it becomes lighter in color). Add the salt, fish sauce, and pepper. Transfer the mixture to a large bowl and set aside.

Add the remaining tablespoon of oil to the same skillet over medium heat, and sauté the bamboo shoot, carrot, and cabbage for 5 minutes or until cooked. Add to the reserved pork mixture and stir to combine. Set aside to cool.

Set a wrapper on a flat surface and place a lettuce leaf in the top center of it, allowing about 1^1/$_2$ inch (3.75 cm) of the lettuce leaf to extend beyond the top of the wrapper. Place about 1 to 2 tablespoons of the pork and vegetable mixture in the middle of the lettuce. Fold the bottom part of the wrapper over half of the filling and then fold the ends toward the middle. Secure the roll using chive stalks (or insert a toothpick). To serve, pour Sweet Garlic Sauce on a roll and top with crushed peanuts.

Serves 4 to 6
Preparation time: 25 minutes
Cooking time: 30 minutes

Sweet Garlic Sauce (page 21)
2 tablespoons oil
3 cloves garlic, crushed with the side of knife and minced
1 onion, minced
^{1}/$_4$ lb (125 g) pork loin or belly (also called "side pork"), diced
^{1}/$_4$ teaspoon salt
1 tablespoon fish sauce
^{1}/$_4$ teaspoon freshly ground black pepper
^{1}/$_2$ cup (130 g) finely chopped bamboo shoots (about one 10-oz (285-g) can)
1 carrot, peeled and cut into thin strips
^{1}/$_4$ lb (125 g) cabbage, thinly shredded
1 head green leaf lettuce
One 16-oz (500-g) package frozen spring roll wrappers (about 8 in/20 cm), thawed
Garlic chives or toothpicks, to secure the rolls
2 tablespoons crushed peanuts

Crispy Fried Fishballs

Everybody in the Philippines loves deep-fried fishballs! They're so popular that there is a street vendor on every corner selling skewers of them with dipping sauces. Their ready availability means that most people don't think of them as something to make at home. I never thought of making fishballs when I was in the Philippines, but since there are no fishball vendors where I live now, the only solution was to try make them. I'm glad I did, because they're fun and easy to make besides being delicious.

Yields about 20 fishballs
Preparation time: 20 minutes + 30 minutes chilling time
Cooking time: 15 minutes

1/2 lb (250 g) white fish fillets (deboned)
1 small onion, minced
1/2 cup (60 g) flour
1 teaspoon salt
1 egg, beaten
2 cups (500 ml) oil for deep-frying (page 18)
Sweet and Spicy Sauce (page 21), Sweet and Sour Sauce (page 21), Sweet Garlic Sauce (page 21) or Garlic Mayonnaise Dip (page 20), for dipping

Carefully check the fish for small bones and then slice it. Place the sliced fish and the onion in a blender or food processor and grind to a paste.

Combine the fish paste with the flour, salt, and egg in a mixing bowl and mix well. Cover and store in a refrigerator for 30 minutes to set.

Scoop out about 1 tablespoon of the fish mixture and shape it into a small ball about 1 in (2.5 cm) across. Continue forming balls with the remainder of the fish mixture.

Heat a small saucepan or wok over high heat and add the oil. Use a wooden chopstick or skewer to check if the oil is hot enough. When it's hot enough, bubbles will form all around the stick. (Or use a deep-fryer thermometer to read the temperature, which should be between 350° and 375°F or 175° and 190°C when ready.) Reduce the heat to medium once it reaches the desired temperature so that the oil doesn't burn. Deep-fry the fishballs over medium heat for about 5 minutes, or until browned. Do not overcrowd the pan. Drain on paper towels. Serve immediately with any of the dips that you like.

Papaya Shrimp Fritters   Ukoy

Filipinos eat Ukoy for a snack or combine them with rice for a complete meal. You may substitute cassava, sweet potato, or bean sprouts for the papaya.

Serves 4 to 6
Preparation time: 20 minutes
Cooking time: 30 minutes

1 medium unripe papaya (1 1/3 lbs/600 g), peeled and grated to make 3 cups (450 g)
2 cups (500 ml) oil for deep-frying (page 18)
1/4 lb (125 g) small fresh shrimp, shell and head on
Spicy Garlic Vinegar Dipping Sauce (page 22), for dipping

Batter
1 cup (112 g) cornstarch
1 cup (125 g) all-purpose flour
1 teaspoon baking powder
1/2 teaspoon salt
1/2 cup (125 ml) annatto water (page 19)
2 eggs, beaten

Combine the ingredients for the Batter and mix thoroughly. Add the papaya and coat it with the Batter.

Heat a medium saucepan or wok over high heat and add the oil. Use a wooden chopstick or skewer to check if the oil is hot enough. When it's hot enough, bubbles will form all around the stick. (Or use a deep-fryer thermometer to read the temperature, which should be between 350° and 375°F or 175° and 190°C when ready.) Reduce the heat to medium once it reaches the desired temperature so that the oil doesn't burn.

Place about 1 1/2 tablespoons of the mixture on a small flat plate or saucer and flatten it into a pancake. Place 2 to 3 small shrimp on top. Gently press the shrimp halfway into the papaya mixture so it doesn't fall off. Carefully slide the pancake into the hot oil. (You can use a round piece of banana leaf to slide the whole mixture into the pan.) Deep fry until crispy and browned. Repeat the process, sliding the papaya and shrimp into the hot oil one by one. Serve with Spicy Garlic Vinegar Dipping Sauce. Add hot steamed rice for an extra hearty snack.

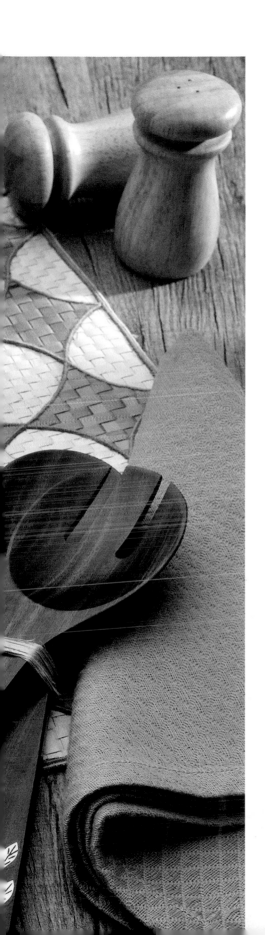

chapter 2
soups

In the Philippines, soup, or *sabaw*, isn't used to start the meals but is normally served as a main dish together with other dishes and steamed rice. That is why Filipino soup dishes are more hearty and never just a plain broth. Sometimes noodles or pasta are added to the soup, such as Noodle Soup with All the Trimmings (page 40) and Macaroni Soup (page 39).

Making Filipino soups is an easy one-step, one-pot process. The most common method to create a stock is to boil chicken or pork in a pot of water (although using bouillon cubes is now common also) and to then add other ingredients and seasonings such as ginger, garlic, tamarind, or fish sauce to form the soup base. In this tropical country, the practice of preparing soup stock beforehand is not common because it takes up valuable space in the refrigerator.

The Philippines is a tropical country with two distinct seasons: wet and dry. From December to February the weather is cooler than usual, though it is still around 68 degrees Fahrenheit (20°C). This is the time of year when soups make a regular appearance on Filipino tables. Soup is a comfort food that warms the body and soothes the soul. When it is scorching hot—as it is much of the time in the Philippines—a light, clear soup like Sinigang Shrimp Soup (page 39) is the more popular choice. Its sour, refreshing taste stimulates the appetite as well as energizes the body. This tamarind-based soup—famous for the variety of different ingredients used to make it, vegetables, shrimp, pork, or beef—is the national soup of the Philippines.

Soup is normally served in a large family-style serving bowl, but it can also be served in individual bowls. Filipinos always eat with a flat plate of steamed rice on the table, so a tasty way to enjoy soup is to spoon it over the rice as a flavoring.

Fish Soup with Miso Dip

Pesang Isda sa Miso

Although whole fish (traditionally *dalag* or snakefish) is used for this dish in the Philippines, any firm-textured white fish fillets or steaks may be used. The fish is boiled with ginger and garlic, and served with an appetizing miso dip. Try using the water from rinsed rice instead of plain water for this soup—Filipinos believe the milky water left over from washing rice contains various nutrients and adds a subtle flavor to the dish.

Cut the fish into 2-inch (5-cm) pieces.

Heat the oil in a skillet over medium heat. Add the garlic and sauté until lightly browned. Add the onion and sauté until translucent.

Bring the water to a boil in a saucepan. Reduce the heat to medium and add the fish, ginger, salt, peppercorn and sautéed garlic and onion. Cover and cook for 10 minutes. Add the cabbage and cook for 5 minutes, or until soft.

To make the Miso Dip, heat the oil in a skillet over medium heat. Add the garlic and sauté until lightly brown. Add the onion and sauté until translucent. Add the tomato, miso, fish sauce, and water. Stir over medium-low heat for 5 minutes. You can serve the dip either at hot or at room temperature.

Serve the soup with the Miso Dip and steamed rice.

Serves 4
Preparation time: 15 minutes
Cooking time: 30 minutes

1 lb (500 kg) white fish fillets or steaks
1 tablespoon oil
3 cloves garlic, crushed with the side of knife
1 onion, sliced
5 cups (1.25 liters) water (preferably rice washing water)
One 2-in (5-cm) piece ginger, peeled and sliced
1$^1/_2$ teaspoons salt
1 teaspoon whole black peppercorns
4 cups (400 g) chopped cabbage (from about $^1/_2$ head cabbage)

Miso Dip
1 tablespoon oil
3 cloves garlic, crushed with the side of knife and minced
1 small onion, sliced thinly
1 tomato, chopped
3 tablespoons miso paste
1 tablespoon fish sauce
4 tablespoons water

Wonton Soup   Pancit Molo

Chinese in origin, Pancit Molo is one of the best-known dishes in the Visayas region of the Philippines. Though the word *pancit* suggests noodles, here Chinese dumplings or wontons are added to a delicious chicken broth. If you don't feel like making the dumplings, you can buy them frozen or just use noodles and bits of chicken meat instead. Wonton wrappers are versatile: You can cut them into small squares and deep-fry them to make delicious chips or you can make ravioli with them.

To make the Dumplings, mix together the pork, shrimp, water chestnuts, salt, and fish sauce in a large bowl. Set a wrapper on a floured flat surface. Place a teaspoon of the pork mixture in the center of the wrapper. Use your finger to moisten the inner edges of the wrapper; this will seal the wonton wrapper together. Gather the four corners of the wrapper toward the center. Make sure there is no air between the wrapper and its filling. Squeeze the corners tightly together to ensure the dumpling stays closed—if the wrapper is loose, the mixture will come out when boiled. Continue filling the other wrappers until all of the pork mixture is used up. You should be able to make about 20 dumplings.

Add oil to a skillet over medium heat and sauté the garlic until lightly browned. Add the onion and sauté until translucent. Set aside.

Add the water and salt to a stockpot, and bring to a boil. Reduce the heat to medium and simmer for 10 minutes. Add the fish sauce, chicken, pepper, garlic, and onion to the broth. Bring to a boil again, and reduce heat to medium. Gently add the wontons to the broth and simmer for 15 minutes.

Ladle the soup and wontons into individual serving bowls. Garnish with the chopped scallions. Serve hot with steamed rice.

Serves 4 to 6
Preparation time: 20 minutes
Cooking time: 1 hour

1 tablespoon oil
3 cloves garlic, crushed with the side of knife and minced
1 onion, minced
8 cups (2 liters) water
1 1/2 teaspoons salt
1 chicken thigh, preferably bone-in, sliced
2 tablespoons fish sauce
1 teaspoon freshly ground black pepper
3 green onions (scallions), finely chopped, for garnish

Dumplings
One 16-oz (454-g) package wonton wrappers
1 lb (500 g) ground pork
1/4 lb (125 g) shrimp, shelled, deveined and sliced
3 water chestnuts, minced
1 teaspoon salt
1 tablespoon fish sauce
4 green onions (scallions), chopped

Sinigang Shrimp Soup

Sinigang Shrimp Soup

There are so many ways to prepare this popular dish. The sour taste comes from unripe or young tamarind pods, but the soup can also be made with guavas, pineapples, unripe tomatoes, or *calamansi* limes instead. Leave the shrimp heads on because they add flavor and aroma to the soup. If you can't find whole fresh or frozen shrimp with the heads still on, opt for shrimp with shells and tails still on. Unlike other soups that warm your body, Sinigang is meant for scorching summer days because the sour taste awakens your tastebuds and stimulates your appetite. This soup is similar to the Thai Tom Yam Kung, but is clear, sweeter, and not as spicy. Shrimp is often used as the main ingredient, but pork, beef, fish, vegetables, or almost anything can be used to make an equally delicious soup.

Serves 4 to 6
Preparation time: 25 minutes
Cooking time: 30 minutes

10 unripe tamarind pods, shelled (or 2 tablespoons tamarind concentrate or 1 packet sinigang powder, page 16)
12 cups (3 liters) water
5 cloves garlic, crushed with the side of knife
1/4 lb (125 g) daikon radish, chopped
One 2-in (5-cm) piece ginger, peeled and sliced
1/4 lb (125 g) taro root (or potato), peeled and cubed
1/4 lb (125 g) okra, trimmed and sliced diagonally
1 tomato, sliced
1 lb (500 g) fresh shrimp, heads and shells on
1/2 lb (250 g) Chinese (Napa) cabbage or bok choy (or spinach), chopped
1 teaspoon salt
5 tablespoons fish sauce (plus extra for dipping if desired)

Boil the shelled tamarind in a saucepan with 4 cups (1 liter) of the water for about 20 minutes until soft. The tamarind has to be submerged. Add more water if necessary. Using a fine-mesh strainer, strain the mixture into a bowl, mashing the pulp with the back of a spoon to force it through the strainer. Discard the pulp and seeds. Set aside the tamarind liquid.

Pour the remaining 8 cups (2 liters) of water into a stockpot, and bring to a boil. Add the garlic, radish, ginger, taro root, and tamarind liquid (or the tamarind concentrate or the sinigang powder) and cook over medium heat for 15 minutes.

Add the okra, tomato, shrimp, Chinese cabbage, and salt, and 5 tablespoons fish sauce and cook for 15 more minutes. Serve hot with steamed rice and fish sauce, if using.

Macaroni Soup
Sopa de Conchitas

This soup uses shell or elbow macaroni and is a Filipino version of minestrone. Popularly known as *sopas*, this comforting home-style soup has a milky pasta broth with chicken, carrots, cabbage, and Vienna sausages added. A fixture on Filipino tables, it can be served as a snack or as a main course with rice or Pan de Sal Bread Rolls (page 30).

Serves 4 to 6
Preparation time: 15 minutes
Cooking time: 45 minutes

2 tablespoons oil
3 cloves garlic, crushed with the side of knife
1 onion, sliced
6 cups (1.5 liters) water
2 chicken thighs, preferably bone-in, sliced
1 1/2 teaspoons salt
1 carrot, peeled and diced
2 cups (250 g) elbow or shell macaroni
3 Vienna sausages, thinly sliced
1/4 lb (125 g) cabbage, thinly sliced
1 teaspoon freshly ground black pepper
1 tablespoon unsalted butter
1 cup (250 ml) milk
4 green onions (scallions), sliced

Heat the oil in a skillet over medium heat. Add the garlic and sauté until lightly browned. Add the onion and sauté until translucent. Set aside.

Add the water to a stockpot and bring to a boil. Add the chicken, salt, and carrot and cook over medium-high heat for 15 minutes, or until the meat is tender. Take the chicken out and tear the meat off the bones using two forks—one to hold the bone and one to tear the meat. Discard the bones. Put the meat back into the stockpot. Add the macaroni, sausages, cabbage, pepper, butter, sautéed onion, and garlic. Simmer over medium-low heat for 15 minutes, or until the macaroni is tender. Pour in the milk and simmer for 5 more minutes.

Ladle the soup into individual bowls, garnish with the green onions and serve immediately.

Noodle Soup with All the Trimmings

Batchoy

This is another signature dish from the Visayas, a group of islands scattered between the main islands of Luzon and Mindanao. Though this rich noodle soup—made with pork, chicken, and shrimp and topped with crushed pork rind—is enjoyed all across the country, the authentic version is found in La Paz, Iloilo Province. This Iloilo version includes egg noodles, whereas other regions leave the noodles out, making a less hearty but nevertheless satisfying meal.

Serves 4 to 6
Preparation time: 30 minutes
Cooking time: 20 minutes

8 cups (2 liters) water
1/3 lb (150 g) bone-in or 1/4 lb (125 g) boneless pork butt or loin
1/4 lb (125 g) pork or chicken liver
1 chicken breast, preferably bone-in
2 tablespoons oil
3 cloves garlic, crushed with the side of knife and minced
1 onion, finely sliced
One 2-in (5-cm) piece ginger, peeled and finely sliced
1/4 lb (125 g) fresh shrimp, shelled and deveined
1 teaspoon salt
1 tablespoon fish sauce
1 tablespoon bottled sautéed shrimp paste (page 16)
1/4 teaspoon sugar
8 oz (240 g) fresh Chinese egg noodles or fettucine or 4 oz (100 g) dried ramen noodles
1/4 teaspoon freshly ground black pepper

Garnishes
4 green onions (scallions), finely sliced
4 tablespoons Fried Garlic (page 23)
1/2 cup (70 g) fried pork rinds, coarsely crushed

Bring the water to a boil in a stockpot. Add the pork, liver, and chicken then cook over high heat for 15 minutes. Skim off the fat.

Using a slotted spoon, remove the pork, chicken, and liver. Reserve the broth. Shred the meat using two forks—one to hold the meat secure on a cutting board and the other to pull the meat into shreds. Slice the liver thinly. Set aside the shredded meat and sliced liver.

Heat the oil in a skillet over medium heat. Add the garlic and sauté until lightly browned. Add the onion and sauté until translucent. Add the ginger and sauté for 3 minutes. Turn off the heat and carefully remove them from the skillet, keeping as much oil in the skillet as possible, and set aside.

In the same skillet, sauté the shredded pork and chicken over medium heat for about 5 minutes, or until lightly browned. Add the shrimp and sauté for 5 minutes more. Set aside.

Add the sautéed garlic and ginger to the broth in the stockpot. Bring to a boil and add the salt, fish sauce, sautéed shrimp paste and sugar. Reduce the heat to medium and add the noodles. Simmer until the noodles are soft—about 10 minutes for dried noodles and 2 to 3 minutes for fresh noodles. Add the pepper.

Ladle the broth and noodles into individual bowls. Top with the sautéed pork and chicken and sliced liver. Sprinkle on the scallions, fried garlic and fried pork rinds. Serve hot.

Noodle Soup with All the Trimmings

Quick Chicken Eggdrop Soup

Misuang Manok

This noodle soup is perfect for chilly weather or for alleviating the effects of a cold. It's quick and easy with relatively few ingredients, but a heartier version could include meatballs, prawns, or mushrooms. Misua is a very fine white Chinese noodle made from wheat flour. Unlike other noodles, misua does not require soaking, but it does cook very quickly, so be careful not to overcook it.

Serves 4
Preparation time: 10 minutes
Cooking time: 30 minutes

1 tablespoon oil
5 cloves garlic, crushed with the side of knife and
  minced
1 onion, sliced thinly
8 cups (2 liters) water
1 chicken breast or thigh, preferably bone-in, sliced
3 tablespoons fish sauce
1 teaspoon salt
$^1/_4$ teaspoon freshly ground black pepper
2 eggs, beaten
4 oz (100 g) dried white wheat noodles (misua)
3 green onions (scallions), minced

Heat the oil in a large saucepan over medium heat and sauté the garlic until lightly browned. Add the onion and sauté until translucent. Add the water and bring to a boil. Add the chicken, fish sauce, salt and pepper and cook over medium heat for 15 minutes.

Add the egg slowly while stirring the soup. Add the noodles and simmer over medium-low heat for 3 minutes, or until soft.

Ladle the soup into individual bowls and garnish with the green onions. Serve immediately.

Chicken Soup with Green Papaya

Tinolang Manok

Serves 4 to 6
Preparation time: 15 minutes
Cooking time: 45 minutes

The fragrant broth of Tinola is the ultimate comfort food that Filipinos crave. This simple, hearty and soothing soup with tender chicken, ginger, papaya, and moringa leaves makes a tasty and healthy meal. Moringa leaves, or *malunggay*, are native to India and contain beta-carotene, vitamin C, and iron. The leaves are used like spinach. Pluck the leaves from the branches just before you cook them. Use baby spinach leaves instead if you cannot find moringa leaves.

2 tablespoons oil

5 cloves garlic, crushed with the side of knife and minced

1 onion, thinly sliced

One 2-in (5-cm) piece ginger, peeled and sliced into strips

4 chicken thighs or breasts, preferably bone-in, cut in halves

1 1/2 teaspoons salt

8 cups (2 liters) water

1 green papaya (or chayote), peeled, deseeded, and cut into bite-size pieces

2 tablespoons fish sauce (plus extra for dipping if desired)

1/2 teaspoon freshly ground black pepper

1/2 cup (50 g) moringa leaves or baby spinach leaves

Heat 1 tablespoon of the oil in a skillet over medium heat and sauté the garlic until lightly browned. Add the onion and ginger and sauté for 10 minutes. Remove from the skillet. Set aside.

Rub the chicken with the salt. To the same skillet, add the remaining 1 tablespoon of oil and set over medium heat. Add the chicken and sauté for 10 minutes, or until lightly browned.

Add the water to a pot and bring to a boil. Add the sautéed chicken, papaya and fish sauce and continue to cook over medium heat for 20 minutes until the papaya is tender. Add the pepper and moringa leaves or spinach. Cover and cook for 5 more minutes.

Serve hot with steamed rice and fish sauce, if using.

Pork and Corn Soup

Nilagang Baboy

You can find this soup of succulent pork, corn, banana, and spinach in a garlic-infused broth on any Filipino table and as a part of the Christmas celebration or on cold, rainy days. It's simple to make and involves a slow cooking process that ensures the meat is tender and the broth is flavorful.

Serves 4 to 6
Preparation time: 15 minutes
Cooking time: 1 hour 15 minutes

1 tablespoon oil
5 cloves garlic, crushed with the side of knife and minced
1 onion, sliced
8 cups (2 liters) water
1 lb (500 g) bone-in or 3/4 lb (750 g) boneless, lean pork (such as chops, loin, center loin roast, loin blade chop), chopped into pieces
1 1/2 teaspoons salt
1 tablespoon whole black peppercorns
2 fresh or frozen ears corn, cut into 2-in (5-cm) lengths
1 potato, peeled and sliced
2 slightly ripe saba bananas (or 1 plantain or 2 unripe regular bananas), sliced
1/2 head green cabbage, roughly chopped
1/4 lb (125 g) spinach, chopped
1 teaspoon sugar
5 tablespoons fish sauce (plus extra for dipping, if desired)

Heat the oil in a skillet over medium heat. Add the garlic and sauté until lightly browned. Add the onion and sauté until translucent. Set aside.

Bring the water to a boil in a stockpot. Add the pork (and any bones), corn and the salt and cook over medium-high heat for 15 minutes. Skim the fat off the broth using a large spoon or ladle.

Add the sautéed garlic and onion, peppercorns, potato, and banana and cook over medium heat for 20 minutes. Add the cabbage, spinach, sugar and fish sauce and cook for 5 more minutes. Serve hot with steamed rice and fish sauce, if using. Remove the cobs before serving, if desired. (Filipinos leave them in for a rustic look!)

> **Tip:** If you're using a bone-in cut of pork, ask your butcher to cut it into pieces for you. Or, if the bone is too daunting to cut through at home, simply cut the meat off the bone and add the bones to the soup during cooking. When cooked, the meat will nearly fall of the bones.

Pork Soup with Squash

Sopas de Upo

For this soup, the pork is first boiled to render the fat, and then sautéed to add a distinct flavor to the meat (this is called "twice cooking"). The garlic and peppercorns give it a surprisingly delicious taste. The vegetable *upo* belongs to the squash family and is also called "long gourd," "upo squash," or "long squash." Native to Africa but widely grown in the tropics and in some European countries, it tastes mostly bland and watery. Zucchini, summer squash, white gourd, chayote, or winter melon make good substitutes. Upo cooks quickly and has a high nutritional value.

Serves 4 to 6
Preparation time: 15 minutes
Cooking time: 55 minutes

2 tablespoons oil
5 cloves garlic, crushed with the side of knife and minced
1 onion, sliced
8 cups (2 liters) water
2 lbs (1 kg) bone-in or 1 1/2 lbs (750 g) boneless pork loin or pork belly (also called "side pork")
1 1/2 teaspoons salt
3 lbs (1.5 kg) long gourd (upo) or other squash or gourd (see suggestions, above), peeled, deseeded, roughly chopped into bite-size pieces
1 tablespoon whole black peppercorns
5 tablespoons fish sauce (plus extra for dipping, if desired)

Heat 1 tablespoon of the oil in a skillet over medium heat. Add the garlic and sauté until lightly browned. Add the onion and sauté until translucent. Set aside.

Add the water to a stockpot and bring to a boil. Add the pork and salt and cook over medium-high heat for 15 minutes. Skim the fat off the top of the broth. Take the pork out of the water using a slotted spoon. Reserve the broth.

Heat the remaining 1 tablespoon of oil in a skillet over medium heat. Add the pork and sauté for 10 minutes, or until lightly browned.

Return the pork to the stockpot. Add the squash, peppercorns, fish sauce and the sautéed garlic and onion. Cook over medium heat for 30 minutes. Serve hot with rice and the fish sauce, if using.

chapter 3
meat dishes

Filipinos love pork, or *baboy*, as much as the Chinese and Spanish do. In fact, many Filipino households in rural areas raise pigs solely for the purpose of selling them to the local butcher or for personal consumption. No part of the pig goes unused—the lungs, heart, face and blood are used to make a variety of delicious dishes while the skin is turned into *chicharon*, or fried pork rinds (page 14). And then there's the iconic whole roasted pig (Litson Baboy) with the famous lechon sauce that's served on holidays and other special occasions. I've included the easier-to-prepare Crispy Lechon Pork (Litson Kawali, page 48) that is also served with the lechon sauce.

The Spanish brought domesticated cattle to the Philippines, but it was the Americans who made beef, or *baka*, popular when they introduced their favorite beef dishes, including steaks and the famous American hamburger. Before the arrival of cows, the traditional beast of burden and source of red meat in the Philippines had been the water buffalo. Still seen pulling plows and carts in the countryside, its meat can be delicious, especially in sausages and corned beef.

Goat meat (*kambing*) is not so common in the Philippines, but in a few regions such as western Mindanao where the Muslim religion prohibits eating pork, it's used more often. Kaldereta Beef Stew (page 53) is a popular way to prepare goat meat.

Regardless of the type of meat used, Filipinos generally marinate their meat to tenderize it and enrich the overall flavor. Make sure you allow enough time to properly marinate your meat, as this is the secret to preparing flavorful meat dishes.

Roasted Marinated Pork

The aroma of grilled pork is always amazing, especially when the pork has been marinated overnight in soy sauce, vinegar, black pepper, sugar and garlic. Grilling the pork gives the dish the distinctive flavor you'll find in Filipino homes. However, grilling isn't always practical or possible, so I often roast the meat in the oven, as this recipe indicates, to get a similar affect. Whichever way you decide to cook it, it's really the marinade that makes this pork so delicious, so plan ahead and marinate the meat the night before.

Serves 4
Preparation time: 10 minutes +
    overnight marinating time
Cooking time: 30 minutes

2 lbs (1 kg) meaty pork spareribs
Vinegar Garlic Sauce (page 20) or Spicy
    Garlic Vinegar Dipping Sauce (page 22), for
    dipping

Marinade
3 cloves garlic, crushed with the side of knife
1 cup (250 ml) Filipino cane vinegar (or white
    vinegar or cider vinegar diluted with water,
    page 13)
2 tablespoons sugar
1 teaspoon salt
3 tablespoons soy sauce
1 teaspoon freshly ground black pepper

Combine the Marinade ingredients in a mixing bowl. Stir until the sugar is dissolved. Arrange the meat in a large casserole dish and pour the marinade over the meat. Cover the dish and keep overnight in the refrigerator.

Preheat the oven to 425°F (220°C). Remove the meat from the marinade. Discard the marinade. Roast the meat for 15 minutes or until browned on top. Turn the meat and continue cooking until it is done (about 15 minutes more).

If you're grilling the ribs, set up a grill for indirect grilling and preheat to medium. Grill the ribs until browned, about 15 minutes, with the grill lid closed. Turn the ribs over and grill for 15 minutes more, with the lid closed.

Slice into serving portions and serve hot with steamed rice and the Vinegar Garlic Sauce or Spicy Garlic Vinegar Dipping Sauce.

Sweet Soy Pork with Black Beans

Humba

Once again, the marinade is the key to this delicious pork recipe. This Visayan dish uses marinated pork belly, which has great flavor and texture, but ham hocks or pork neck will also work. The marinated meat is simmered for nearly an hour until all the liquid is gone making the meat melt-in-the-mouth tender. This dish is also called *Adobong Visaya* or *Humba*, derived from the Chinese word meaning "red braised meat." Adding the fermented black beans to the sauce brings an additional pungency to the pork.

Serves 4
Preparation time: 15 minutes
  + overnight marinating time
Cooking time: 1 hour

2 lbs (1 kg) pork belly (also called "side pork") or shoulder, cut into serving pieces
3 tablespoons bottled or canned fermented black beans or black bean sauce

Marinade
3 cloves garlic, crushed with the side of knife
1/2 cup (125 ml) Filipino cane vinegar (or white vinegar or cider vinegar diluted with water, page 13)
1/2 cup (100 g) brown sugar
3 tablespoons soy sauce
1 teaspoon salt
1 teaspoon whole black peppercorns
2 cups (500 ml) water
1 bay leaf

Combine the Marinade ingredients in a mixing bowl. Stir until the sugar is dissolved. Pour the Marinade over the meat. Cover and keep overnight in the refrigerator.

Transfer the meat and marinade to a saucepan and bring to a boil over high heat. Reduce the heat to medium-low and simmer until the meat is tender, for about 50 minutes. Add the black beans and simmer until most of the liquid has evaporated, about 10 minutes. Serve hot with steamed rice.

Crispy Lechon Pork

Litson Kawali

While Litson (or Lechon) Baboy refers to the whole roasted pig that is served for fiestas and special occasions, Litson Kawali is an everyday dish that Filipinos love to cook and eat. The pork is first simmered for twenty minutes and then it is flash-fried in oil to give it a crunch. Sometimes, I'll fry it the day before I serve it and then fry it one more time just before it's served to make it even crunchier. It's the Lechon Sauce that makes this dish a Filipino favorite.

Place the pork and water in a large saucepan, bring to a boil. Add the garlic, bay leaf, pepper and salt and cook over medium heat for 20 minutes or until the meat is done. Drain the pork and discard the water and discard the water. Pat the pork dry with paper towels, and cut into serving pieces.

Heat a small saucepan or wok over high heat and add the oil. Use a wooden chopstick or skewer to check if the oil is hot enough. When it's hot enough, bubbles form all around the stick. (Or use a deep-fryer thermometer to read the temperature, which should be between 350° and 375°F or 175° and 190°C when ready.) Reduce the heat to medium once it reaches the desired temperature so that the oil doesn't burn. Add a couple of pieces of pork at a time and deep-fry until brown and crispy. Do not overcrowd the pan. Blisters should appear on the skin. Remove the pork and drain on paper towels.

Make the Liver Paste for the Lechon Sauce, following the recipe on page 23.

To make the Lechon Sauce, heat a saucepan or skillet over medium heat and add the oil and garlic. Sauté the garlic until lightly browned. Add the Liver Paste, sugar, vinegar, water, soy sauce, salt and pepper and simmer over medium heat for 10 minutes or until the sauce thickens. Serve the pork with the Lechon Sauce and hot steamed rice.

Serves 4 to 6
Preparation time: 20 minutes
Cooking time: 30 minutes

2 lbs (1 kg) pork belly (or "side pork") or shoulder, preferably with skin on
8 cups (2 liters) water
3 cloves garlic, crushed with the side of knife
1 bay leaf
1 teaspoon freshly ground black pepper
1 teaspoon salt
2 cups (500 ml) oil, for deep-frying

Lechon Sauce (Makes about 1 1/2 cups/ 375 ml)
1 cup (200 g) Liver Paste (page 23)
1 tablespoon oil
3 cloves garlic, crushed with the side of knife and minced
1 tablespoon sugar
3 tablespoons Filipino cane vinegar (or white vinegar or cider vinegar diluted with water, page 13)
3 tablespoons water
1 tablespoon soy sauce
1 teaspoon salt
1/2 teaspoon freshly ground black pepper

Glazed Christmas Ham with Pineapple

Hamon

An elegant roasted ham, or *hamon*, is the centerpiece of a Filipino family's Christmas Eve dinner. Hamon is simple to make and impressive in its presentation—especially when garnished with fresh pineapple slices. After everyone has had their fill, the leftovers can be used in other dishes like Chicken Stew with Vegetables (page 66) or in delicious sandwiches made with Pan de Sal Bread Rolls (page 30).

Serves 8
Preparation time: 25 minutes
Cooking time: 1 hour 25 minutes

5 lbs (2.25 kg) smoked bone-in ham leg
8 cups (2 liters) pineapple juice
2 cups (400 g) brown sugar
$1/2$ cup (125 ml) water
$1/2$ lb (250 g) peeled, cored and sliced fresh pineapple (from about $1/2$ pineapple) or one 20-oz (567-g) canned pineapple slices, for garnish

Place the ham, pineapple juice, and 1 cup (200 g) of the brown sugar in a stockpot. The ham should be submerged in the juice. Add more juice or some water to cover, if necessary. Bring to a boil and then reduce the heat to medium and cook for 1 hour. The skin should come off easily when the ham is done. Drain and set aside to cool.

Preheat the oven to 400°F (200°C).

To make the glaze, place the remaining 1 cup (200 g) of brown sugar and the water in a small saucepan. Bring to a boil over medium heat and cook for 3 minutes while stirring constantly.

Place the ham on a baking tray, score the top of the ham in a crisscross pattern using a knife. Brush on the glaze and bake for 20 minutes or until browned.

Garnish with the pineapple pieces and serve.

Fiery Pork Stew with Coconut

Bicol Express

This is the signature dish of the Bicol Province in the Southeastern part of Luzon, a cuisine known for its generous use of hot chili peppers and coconut milk. One teaspoonful of this spicy recipe will send you running for a glass of water like an "express train." Reducing the amount of chili peppers will lower the "heat" if you're not into spicy food, but if you like your food hot then this is the perfect dish for you. Filipino farmers love this dish because it gives them an energy boost before they spend the day under the scorching Philippine sun.

Serves 4 to 6
Preparation time: 10 minutes
Cooking time: 30 minutes

2 tablespoons oil
3 cloves garlic, crushed with the side of knife and minced
1 onion, sliced
1 tomato, sliced
2 lbs (1 kg) pork butt or belly (also called "side pork"), cut into bite-size pieces
$1/2$ teaspoon salt
One $13 1/2$-oz (400-ml) can coconut milk
4 to 6 finger-length green chili peppers, deseeded and thinly sliced
1 tablespoon bottled sautéed shrimp paste (page 16)

Heat a skillet over high heat and add the oil. Add the garlic and sauté until lightly browned. Add the onion and tomato, and sauté until the onion is translucent.

Add the remaining 1 tablespoon of oil, the pork and salt, and sauté over medium heat for 10 minutes, or until lightly browned. Add the coconut milk and bring to a boil. Lower the heat to medium and cook for 15 minutes. Add the chili peppers and cook 5 minutes more. Remove from the heat and stir in the sautéed shrimp paste. Serve hot with steamed rice.

Traditional Tocino Bacon

It takes a full week for this bacon to cure, but the results are amazing. In this Kapampangan version of the dish, all you need is salt and sugar, and then let time do its work in curing the pork into a sweet-tasting, heavenly dish. Tocino is one-third of the Filipino popular breakfast meal called *Tosilog*—an acronym for <u>To</u>cino, <u>Si</u>nangag (fried rice), and Pritong It<u>log</u> (fried egg). Placing the meat in the freezer until it's partially frozen will make it easier to cut.

Combine the salt and sugar in a mixing bowl and mix thoroughly. Dredge each meat slice in the mixture. Place in an airtight container and store in the refrigerator for about 1 week.

To cook the meat, place the water and cured meat in a large skillet, and bring to a boil. Stir the meat over medium heat until the water evaporates, about 10 minutes. Add the oil and fry over low heat to your liking. Serve hot with Fried Rice with Egg (page 91) and 1 fried egg per person.

Serves 4 to 6
Preparation time: 15 minutes + 1 week storing time
Cooking time: 15 minutes

1 tablespoon salt
1/2 cup (50 g) sugar
2 lbs (1 kg) boneless pork belly or shoulder, sliced
3 cups (750 ml) water
1 tablespoon oil
Fried Rice with Egg (page 91)
4–6 fried eggs (1 egg per person)

Pork and Tomato Stew Menudo

Serves 4 to 6
Preparation time: 35 minutes
Cooking time: 45 minutes

Some Filipinos believe that Menudo will cure a hangover, and whether that is true or not, this hearty dish will definitely satisfy a craving for meat. Menudo means "small" and so the pork in this dish is sliced into bite-size pieces. Unlike the spicy Mexican Menudo, this version is milder and sweeter.

Rinse the pork and liver and cut into bite-size cubes. Place the cubed meat in a saucepan, cover with water, and bring to gentle boil over medium heat. Boil for 10 minutes and then drain the meat well (discard the cooking liquid).

Heat a skillet over medium heat and add the oil. Add the garlic and sauté until lightly brown. Add the onion and sauté until translucent. Add the meat and liver and fry until lightly brown. Add the remaining 1 tablespoon of oil, carrot, potato, fish sauce, and cook over medium heat for 15 minutes, stirring frequently.

Add the green and red bell pepper, chickpeas, tomato, tomato sauce, paprika, water, and soy sauce. Cover and cook over medium heat for 20 minutes or until the meat is tender. Stir occasionally.

Add the raisins, salt and pepper, and simmer for 5 more minutes. Serve hot with steamed rice.

1 lb (450 g) bone-in, pork belly (also called "side pork") or loin, rinsed and cut into cubes
1/4 lb (110 g) pork or chicken liver, rinsed and cut into cubes
2 tablespoons oil
3 cloves garlic, crushed with the side of knife
1 onion, diced
1 carrot, peeled and diced
1 potato, peeled and diced
1 tablespoon fish sauce
1 green bell pepper, deseeded and diced
1 red bell pepper, deseeded and diced
One 15-oz (420-g) can chickpeas, drained
1 tomato, chopped
One 8-oz (227-g) can tomato sauce
1/2 teaspoon paprika
1 tablespoon water
1 tablespoon soy sauce
1/2 cup (70 g) raisins
1/2 teaspoon salt
1/4 teaspoon freshly ground black pepper

Filipino Beefsteak

Filipino Beefsteak

This dish is called *Bistek* in the Philippines, which comes from the Spanish word bistec or "beefsteak." The recipe calls for first marinating the meat in soy sauce, lime juice and black pepper, and then sautéeing it with garlic and onion, which tenderizes the meat and adds a delicious aroma and flavor. Because Filipinos do not use a knife at the table, Bistek is not served as a large slab of steak but is always thinly sliced. This luscious and quick meal is always a big hit with my friends and family.

Combine the Marinade ingredients in a large mixing bowl. Stir until the sugar is dissolved. Add in the meat, and toss to coat. Marinate the meat in the refrigerator for at least 3 hours or overnight. Reserve the marinade.

Heat a skillet over medium heat and add the oil. Add the garlic and sauté until lightly browned. Add the onion and sauté for 2 minutes. Remove half of the onion and set aside to be used for garnish later. Add the meat and sauté for about 10 minutes. Pour in the reserved marinade and simmer over medium heat for another 10 minutes.

Place the beef on a serving platter and garnish with the reserved onion and pineapple, if using. Serve hot with steamed rice.

Serves 4 to 6
Preparation time: 15 minutes + marinating time
Cooking time: 30 minutes

2 lbs (1 kg) beef sirloin or London broil, sliced

2 tablespoons oil

7 cloves garlic, crushed with the side of knife and minced

1 onion, cut into rings

1/2 lb (250 g) peeled, cored and sliced fresh pineapple (from about 1/2 pineapple) or one 20-oz (567-g) can pineapple slices or chunks (optional), for garnish

Marinade

1 tablespoon sugar

1/2 cup (125 ml) freshly squeezed calamansi or lime juice

1/2 cup (125 ml) soy sauce

1 teaspoon salt

1/2 teaspoon freshly ground black pepper

Kaldereta Beef Stew

A specialty of Pampanga province, this rich beef stew has potatoes, green peas, carrot, and bell pepper simmered in a flavorful tomato sauce. The sauce-thickening agent is liver paste which adds a distinctive flavor to the dish. This stew is traditionally made with goat meat and served during fiesta time when a whole goat is slaughtered to feed a large number of people. It is equally delicious prepared with lamb, pork, or chicken. Whichever meat you choose, this makes a great one-pot meal.

Make the Liver Paste, following the recipe on page 23.

Heat a skillet over medium heat, add the oil and sauté the garlic until lightly browned. Add the onion and sauté until translucent. Add the meat and sauté for about 10 minutes.

In a large saucepan over medium heat, add the sautéed meat, garlic, onion, as well as the water, salt, pepper, and vinegar. Cook for about 10 minutes, stirring frequently.

Add the chili pepper, bay leaf, bell pepper, potato, carrot, green peas, tomato, sugar, tomato sauce and Liver Paste. Bring to a boil. Reduce the heat to medium-low and simmer for 1 hour or until the meat is tender.

Place on a serving bowl and top with grated cheese, if using. Serve with steamed rice.

Serves 4
Preparation time: 15 minutes
Cooking time: 1 hour 30 minutes

1 cup (200 g) Liver Paste (page 23)

1 tablespoon oil

3 cloves garlic, crushed with the side of knife

1 onion, sliced

1 lb (500 g) beef shank or chuck, cut into bite-size pieces

2 cups (500 ml) water

1/2 tablespoon salt

1 teaspoon freshly ground black pepper

3 tablespoons Filipino cane vinegar (or white vinegar or cider vinegar diluted with water, page 13)

1 finger-length green chili pepper, deseeded and minced

1 bay leaf

1 small bell pepper, deseeded and sliced

1 potato, peeled and diced

1 small carrot, peeled and diced

1/2 cup (75 g) fresh or frozen green peas

1 tomato, sliced

1 teaspoon sugar

One 8-oz (227-g) can tomato sauce

1/2 cup (50 g) grated cheddar cheese (optional)

Marinated Morcon Stuffed Beef Roll Morcon

In Spain, cured sausage is used to stuff this dish, but people of the Philippines make it with carrots, pickles, Vienna sausages, cheese, and eggs. The filling of this dish is rolled into a large sheet of marinated flank steak (about ¼-inch or 6-mm thick) and tied with twine before being simmered in a flavorful tomato-based sauce. Your butcher can cut the flank steak to the right size, or if you can't find one large piece of meat, then use two pieces at least 8 inches (20 cm) wide.

Serves 4
Preparation time: 20 minutes +
  marinating time
Cooking time: 55minutes

About 2 lbs (1 kg) flank steak, depending on the size of the steak cut into one large ¼-in (6-mm)-thick sheet or multiple smaller sheets at least 8 in (20 cm) wide
One 5-oz (142-g) can Vienna sausages
1 carrot, peeled and cut into ½-in (1.25-cm) strips
¼ cup (100 g) sweet gherkin pickles, sliced into strips
2 thin slices cheddar cheese (about ⅛-in/3-mm thick)
2 hard-boiled eggs, quartered
2 tablespoons all-purpose flour
2 tablespoons oil
Kitchen twine
3 cloves garlic, crushed with the side of knife
1 small onion, minced
1 cup (250 ml) water
1 bay leaf
One 8-oz (227-g) can tomato sauce
1 teaspoon freshly ground black pepper
1 teaspoon salt
4 tablespoons soy sauce

Marinade
2 tablespoons soy sauce
1 teaspoon salt
½ teaspoon freshly ground black pepper
½ cup (125 ml) freshly squeezed calamansi or lime juice

Combine the Marinade ingredients in a small bowl. Place the beef in a casserole dish and pour the marinade over the meat, turning the beef to coat evenly. Marinate the beef in the refrigerator for at least 1 hour. Reserve the marinade.

Form the beef roll following the steps shown below.

Heat a skillet over medium heat and add the oil. Add the beef roll and brown it on all sides, about 5 minutes. Remove the meat and set aside.

Heat a large skillet over medium heat and add the remaining 1 tablespoon of oil. Add the garlic and sauté until lightly browned. Add the onion and sauté until translucent. Add the reserved marinade, water, bay leaf, tomato sauce, pepper, salt, and soy sauce and cook over medium heat for 5 minutes, stirring occasionally. Add the beef roll and cover. Simmer over medium-low heat for about 45 minutes—remember to turn the beef roll occasionally—or until it is cooked. Remove the beef roll.

Remove the twine and slice the beef roll into several disks. Place the sliced beef roll on a serving platter and spoon the sauce over it. Serve hot with steamed rice.

How to make the Stuffed Beef Roll

1 Lay the meat on a large platter with the shorter end facing you. Place the slices of Vienna sausage, carrot, pickles, cheese, and egg on the end near you.

2 Roll up the beef up tightly and tie with the twine. Roll the meat in the flour to coat it evenly.

Oxtail Vegetable Stew

Kare-Kare

This thick stew makes a hearty meal with an unusual combination of flavors. Eggplant and green beans in a savory peanut butter sauce accent the meaty goodness of delectable oxtails. Oxtails might be hard to find, or rather expensive, in which case you can substitute beef shank or short ribs, or even pork. Some people use unsweetened peanut butter, but I like the tang of the more common sweetened peanut butter. Serve it with rice and some *bagoong* for dipping.

Serves 4
Preparation time: 20 minutes
Cooking time: 1 hour

1¼ lbs (600 g) oxtail (or beef shank or ribs)
6 cups (1.5 liters) water
2 teaspoons salt
2 tablespoons uncooked white rice (or store-bought rice flour)
2 tablespoons oil
3 cloves garlic, crushed with the side of knife
1 onion, sliced
½ cup (125 ml) annatto water (see page 19) (optional)
4 tablespoons bottled peanut butter
½ lb (225 g) green beans, trimmed and cut into 2-in (5-cm) lengths
1 lb (400 g) eggplant, trimmed and sliced
1 head Chinese (Napa) cabbage), chopped, or 2 bunches spinach, rinsed and trimmed
2 tablespoons bottled sautéed shrimp paste (page 16)

Slice the oxtail into ½-inch (1.25-cm) pieces or cut the beef into cubes. Place the meat in a saucepan. Add the water and 1 teaspoon of the salt and bring to a boil. Cook over medium heat for 15 minutes or until the meat becomes tender. Skim the fat from the top of the broth. Set aside and reserve the broth.

Place the rice in a small skillet and stir over medium heat for 10 minutes or until lightly browned. Place toasted rice in a mortar or food processor and grind to a flourlike consistency. If you're using pre-ground rice flour, place the flour in small skillet and lightly brown over medium heat, about 5 minutes, stirring frequently. Set aside.

Heat a skillet over medium heat and add the oil. Add the garlic and sauté until lightly browned. Add the onion and sauté until translucent. Add the meat and the remaining 1 teaspoon of salt. Cook until lightly browned.

In a saucepan, add 4 cups (1 liter) of the reserved broth, the annatto water, if using, peanut butter, toasted rice flour, green beans, and eggplant and cook over medium heat for 20 minutes or until tender, stirring occasionally. Add the Chinese cabbage and simmer over medium-low heat for 5 minutes. Serve hot with steamed rice and sautéed shrimp paste.

Oxtail Vegetable Stew

Stuffed Meatloaf with Cheese and Sausage
Embutido

The Filipino version of Embutido, which means "sausage" is a steamed meatloaf made with ground pork, bell peppers, raisins, hardboiled eggs, and cheese. (The original Spanish version of this dish is really a kind of sausage and more like the Filipino *longganisa*.) You can make these colorful meatloafs over the weekend, keep them in the refrigerator, and serve a few days later, or even a week later if you freeze them. They taste delicious chilled or fried.

Serves 6
Preparation time: 30 minutes
Cooking time: 1 1/2 hours

2 lbs (1 kg) ground pork or beef
1 carrot, peeled and grated
1 bell pepper, deseeded and grated
1/2 cup (70 g) raisins
1 cup (100 g) grated cheddar cheese
1 tablespoon salt
1 teaspoon freshly ground black pepper
1 teaspoon cornstarch
6 sheets heavy duty aluminum foil, each about 12 x 15 in (30 x 38 cm)
3 hard-boiled eggs, cut into wedges
One 5-oz (142-g) can Vienna sausages
Banana ketchup or tomato ketchup, for dipping

Mix the ground pork or beef, carrot, bell pepper, raisins, cheese, salt, pepper, and cornstarch in a large bowl. Mix thoroughly with a wooden spoon. Divide the mixture into 6 equal portions.

Spread one portion of the meat mixture on a sheet of heavy duty aluminum foil and flatten. Place 2 or 3 egg wedges and a Vienna sausage in the middle of the mixture. Roll up the mixture by bringing up the foil and pressing the mixture. Make sure that the meat mixture covers the eggs and sausage. Be careful not to roll the foil inside the meat when rolling it up. Tightly twist both ends to seal them shut (like the ends of a Tootsie Roll). If not tightly wrapped, the meat will crumble when the foil is opened.

Arrange the meatloafs in a steamer and cook for 1 hour. Set aside to cool for at least 20 minutes before unwrapping and slicing the rolls.

Slice across into 1/2-inch disks and arrange onto a serving platter. Serve with steamed rice and banana ketchup or tomato ketchup on the side.

chapter 4
poultry dishes

When in the Philippines, one is almost always awakened by the crowing of early-rising roosters. Clucking hens and chirping chicks provide an auditory backdrop to a typical day in the Filipino countryside. Chickens are found roaming all over the Philippines providing their owners with a fresh eggs and meat. Like the pig, no part of the chicken, or *manok*, goes to waste. Street vendors offer a broad and unusual selection of colorfully named chicken parts: grilled chicken heads (Filipinos nickname this street food the "helmet"), grilled chicken feet (called "adidas"), and grilled intestines (or "IUD").

Chicken is a great vehicle to absorb the flavors of spices and seasonings, and it cooks relatively quickly. Specific cuts of chicken are used in different dishes; however, most are bone-in pieces for the additional flavor that the bones provide.

One of the all-time favorite Filipino dishes is Chicken Adobo (page 64). Because it uses a great deal of vinegar, it keeps for a couple of days without refrigeration, and the taste gets better and better the longer it is kept as the sauce and spices penetrate the meat. One whiff of this familiar dish will make any Filipino expatriate nostalgic for his or her homeland.

Another classic chicken dish is Pochero (Chicken Stew with Vegetables, page 66). It is a one-pot stew that uses any kind of meat—chicken, ham, chorizo, beef, or pork—and vegetables, although chicken is the most common main ingredient. This is usually prepared on Sundays for lunch in many Filipino households.

Also included in this chapter is Barbecued Chicken Skewers (page 61), which are always served at parties and family get-togethers. The chicken is marinated in limejuice and a lemon-lime soda pop, providing a subtle, sweet flavor that also tenderizes the meat.

Chicken and Vegetables in Tangy Tomato Sauce

Afritadang Manok

In this dish, juicy chicken is first stir-fried and then slow-braised with bell peppers and potatoes in a tomato-based sauce. *Fritada* means "fried" in Spanish and manok is "chicken" in Tagalog. Variations of this dish are found throughout the Philippines. Any part of the chicken can be used but Filipinos generally prefer to cook with bone-in meat as it is more flavorful. This recipe works great with pork, beef or fish.

Serves 4
Preparation time: 15 minutes
Cooking time: 50 minutes

2 tablespoons oil
3 cloves garlic, crushed with the side of knife and minced
1 onion, minced
2 lbs (1 kg) skinless bone-in chicken pieces (breasts, thighs or drumsticks)
1 teaspoon salt
1 potato, peeled and diced
1 cup (250 ml) water
1 bay leaf
1 tomato, diced
One 8-oz (227-g) can tomato sauce
$^1/_2$ cup (75 g) fresh or frozen green peas
1 tablespoon fish sauce
1 bell pepper, deseeded and diced
1 teaspoon sugar
$^1/_4$ teaspoon freshly ground black pepper

Heat a large skillet over medium heat and add 1 tablespoon of the oil. Add the garlic and sauté until lightly browned. Add the onion and sauté until translucent. Remove the garlic and onion, and reserve.

Rub the chicken pieces with the salt. Add the remaining 1 tablespoon of oil to the same skillet over medium heat and sauté the chicken until lightly browned, about 15 minutes.

Place the potato and water in a saucepan and bring to a boil. Reduce the heat to medium. Add the sautéed chicken, garlic, onion, bay leaf, tomato, tomato sauce, green peas, fish sauce, bell pepper, and sugar. Cover and simmer over medium to low heat for 30 minutes, or until tender. Add ground black pepper and simmer for 3 more minutes. Serve hot with steamed rice.

Chicken and Vegetables in Tangy Tomato Sauce

Barbecued Chicken Skewers
Inihaw na Manok

Marinated chunks of chicken are threaded on bamboo skewers and grilled over an open fire or under a broiler in the oven or oven-roasted. In this recipe, the meat is usually seasoned with a sweet garlic marinade before grilling. Soda pop added to the marinade gives the meat a sweet flavor and tenderizes it too. When I cook this dish, I always make double portions. The leftovers are perfect for the next day's lunch box and because it freezes well, it makes a great "instant meal." Also try it using pork, any vegetable or seafood.

Serves 6
Preparation time: 10 minutes + 3 hours marinating time
Cooking time: 30 minutes

2 lbs (1 kg) boneless, skinless chicken breasts or thighs
12 to 15 bamboo skewers, soaked in water for 30 minutes prior to grilling or roasting
Vinegar Garlic Sauce (page 20) or Sweet and Spicy Sauce (page 21), for dipping

Marinade
1 cup (250 ml) soy sauce
1/3 cup (80 ml) freshly squeezed calamansi or lime juice
5 cloves garlic, crushed with the side of knife
1 onion, minced
One 12-oz (355-ml) can Sprite or 7-Up
1 tablespoon sugar
1 tablespoon salt
1 teaspoon freshly ground black pepper

Cut the chicken into 1-inch (2-cm) cubes. Combine the Marinade ingredients in a mixing bowl and mix thoroughly. Add the chicken pieces and coat them well, then place in the refrigerator for at least 3 hours or overnight. Reserve the liquid to use as basting sauce.

Thread 5 or 6 pieces of meat onto each skewer. To grill the skewers, set up a grill for direct grilling and preheat to medium to high heat. To broil the skewers in the oven, turn the broiler to high and set the oven rack 3 to 5 inches (7.5 to 12.75 cm) from the heat source. Grill or broil the chicken for a total of about 10 minutes, turning frequently and basting with the leftover Marinade.

To oven roast the skewers, preheat the oven to 400°F (200°C). Cook the chicken for about 20 minutes, turning frequently and basting with the leftover Marinade. The chicken is done when it has turned golden brown and crispy at the edges, but be careful not overcook it. Serve hot with Vinegar Garlic Sauce or Sweet and Spicy Sauce and steamed rice.

Coconut Chicken with Pineapple

Pininyahang Manok

Serves 4
Preparation time: 15 minutes
Cooking time: 30 minutes

2 tablespoons oil
3 cloves garlic, crushed with the side of
  knife
1 onion, sliced
1½ lbs (750 g) boneless, skinless
  chicken breasts, thighs or drumsticks,
  cut into cubes
1 teaspoon salt
1 tomato, diced
One 13½-oz (400-ml) can coconut milk
2½ cups (250 g) fresh or canned
  pineapple, cubed
1 tablespoon fish sauce

Filipino children love this dish. The tender pieces of chicken and the sweet
pineapple chunks float in a creamy bath of coconut milk. This savory and
sweet combination produces a dish that people of all ages will love. This
recipe demonstrates the flexibility of pineapple, a fruit that is used for a
main dish as well as a part of a dessert. Evaporated milk can be a convenient
substitute for coconut milk.

Heat a skillet over medium heat and add 1 tablespoon of the oil. Add the garlic and sauté until
lightly browned. Add the onion and sauté until translucent. Remove the sautéed garlic and onion,
and set aside.

  Toss the chicken cubes with the salt. To the same skillet over medium-high heat, add the
remaining 1 tablespoon of the oil. Stir-fry the chicken for about 15 minutes or until lightly browned.
Add the garlic and onion.

  Add the tomato, coconut milk and pineapple and simmer over medium-low heat for 10 minutes.
Season with the fish sauce. Serve hot with steamed rice.

Tangy Asado Chicken

With a beautiful contrast of textures and colors, this Filipino Asado is a moderately spicy chicken dish simmered in tomatoes and Filipino cane vinegar. Its origins are Chinese, and it highlights the best of Comida China in Philippine cuisine. The pork or beef version is used as a filling for steamed buns, called *siopao*, another Chinese legacy.

Heat a skillet over medium heat and add 1 tablespoon of the oil. Add the garlic and sauté until lightly browned. Add the onion and sauté until translucent. Remove from the skillet and set aside.

Rub the chicken with the salt. To the same skillet over medium heat, add the remaining 1 tablespoon of oil and sauté the chicken until lightly browned, about 10 minutes. Set aside.

In a large saucepan, add the tomatoes, chili pepper, bay leaf, vinegar, and water and bring to a boil. Reduce heat to medium. Add the sautéed chicken, garlic, onion, paprika, pepper, and soy sauce and cook for 20 minutes, or until tender. Serve hot with steamed rice.

Serves 4
Preparation time: 15 minutes
Cooking time: 35 minutes

2 tablespoons oil
3 cloves garlic, crushed
1 onion, finely sliced
2 to 2^1/$_2$ lbs (1 to 1.25 kg) bone-in chicken pieces (breast, thighs, and/or drumsticks)
1 teaspoon salt
2 tomatoes, sliced
1 finger-length green chili pepper, minced
1 bay leaf
3 tablespoons Filipino cane vinegar (or cider vinegar diluted with water, page 13)
^{1}/$_2$ cup (125 ml) water
1 tablespoon paprika
^{1}/$_4$ teaspoon freshly ground black pepper
1 tablespoon soy sauce

Chicken Adobo

Adobo is, hands down, the most popular dish in the Philippines. The local favorites are Chicken Adobo and Pork Adobo, although Adobo can also be made using seafood, beef, or vegetables. Marinating the meat overnight in the vinegar marinade results in a rich flavor and smooth texture. Prepare the dish a day before and then reheat it the next day for a thicker sauce and a more robust flavor. Served with a large bowl of steamed rice, Adobo's soy sauce and vinegar combination can be addictive. Vinegar inhibits spoilage, so Adobo can be kept for a few days without refrigeration. (Avoid using an aluminum saucepan when cooking Adobo as the vinegar will react chemically with the aluminum and change the taste of the dish. Cast iron, enameled cast iron, or stainless-steel pans are better choices.)

Serves 4
Preparation time: 5 minutes + overnight marinating time
Cooking time: 1 hour

$2^1/_2$ lbs (1.25 kg) bone-in chicken breasts, thighs or drumsticks
1 tablespoon oil
3 cloves garlic, crushed with the side of knife
1 teaspoon whole black peppercorns
1 teaspoon brown sugar
1 bay leaf
1 large onion, sliced into rings

Adobo Marinade
1 cup (250 ml) Filipino cane vinegar (or white vinegar or cider vinegar diluted with water, page 13)
$^1/_4$ cup (65 ml) freshly squeezed calamansi or lime juice
1 cup (250 ml) soy sauce

Combine the Marinade ingredients in a mixing bowl and mix thoroughly. Add the chicken and store overnight in the refrigerator.

Remove the chicken from the Marinade. Reserve the Marinade.

Heat a skillet over medium heat and add the oil. Add the garlic and sauté until lightly browned. Add the chicken and sauté for 10 minutes.

Add the Marinade, peppercorns, sugar, and bay leaf. Cover the pan and bring to a boil. Reduce the heat to medium-low. Simmer until the meat is tender, 45 minutes or more. Add the onion and simmer 5 minutes more. Serve hot with steamed rice.

Chicken Adobo

Filipino Fried Chicken
Pritong Manok

This Filipino–style fried chicken is crispy on the outside and juicy and moist on the inside. What brings out the flavor in this otherwise common dish are the spices and vinegar that seep into the chicken when they are simmered together. Frying the chicken locks the juice inside. This classic is really tasty when served with banana ketchup or a vinegar-based dipping sauce—try Vinegar Garlic Sauce (page 20).

Serves 4
Preparation time: 15 minutes
Cooking time: 30 minutes

1/2 cup (125 ml) Filipino cane vinegar (or white vinegar or cider vinegar diluted with water, page 13)
4 cups (1 liter) water
5 cloves garlic, crushed
1 bay leaf
1/2 cup (125 ml) soy sauce
1 tablespoon freshly ground black pepper
1 tablespoon salt
2 lbs (1 kg) bone-in, skin-on, chicken breasts, thighs, drumsticks or wings
1 cup (125 g) all-purpose flour
3 cups (750 ml) oil for deep-frying (page 18)
Vinegar Garlic Sauce (page 20) or banana ketchup, for dipping

In a saucepan, place the vinegar, water, garlic, bay leaf, soy sauce, pepper and 1/2 tablespoon of salt. Bring to a boil and then add the chicken. Cook over high heat for 10 minutes. Drain and pat dry with paper towels.

Place the flour and remaining 1/2 tablespoon of the salt in a mixing bowl. Add the chicken and coat the pieces evenly.

Heat a saucepan or wok over high heat, and add the oil. Use a wooden chopstick or skewer to check if the oil is hot enough. When it's hot enough, bubbles will form all around the stick. (Or use a deep-fryer thermometer to read the temperature, which should be between 350° and 375°F or 175° and 190°C when ready.) Reduce the heat to medium once it reaches the desired temperature so that the oil doesn't burn.

Deep-fry the chicken pieces for about 15 minutes or until lightly browned. Do not overcrowd the pan. Serve hot with steamed rice and banana ketchup or Vinegar Garlic Sauce.

Chicken Stew with Vegetables

Pochero

Filipino Pochero is similar to Spanish Cocido, a stew of chicken, sausage and vegetables. The Filipino version, however, uses a delicious garlic and eggplant sauce that sets it apart. This is a regular Sunday meal and, in some households, it is made right after Christmas when there are plenty of leftovers. Variations are found all across the country. Adding beef or pork creates a wonderfully meaty stew.

To make the Eggplant Sauce, boil the eggplant over high heat for 5 minutes or until soft. Cut off the stem end, peel the skin and mash the flesh. Combine the mashed eggplant, garlic, vinegar, salt, and pepper in a saucepan and simmer over medium-low heat for 3 minutes. Set aside.

Place the chicken, chorizo, ham, salt and 5 cups (1.25 liters) water in a saucepan and bring to a boil. Reduce heat to medium and cook for 30 minutes, or until the meat is tender. Remove the meat with a slotted spoon. Set the saucepan and broth aside.

Heat a skillet over medium heat, add the oil. Add the garlic and sauté until lightly browned. Set aside.

Add the chickpeas, potato, banana, and garlic to the saucepan with the chicken and ham broth. Cook over medium-high heat for about 10 minutes, or until soft. With a slotted spoon, remove the chickpeas, potato, and bananas, and set aside. Add the cabbage and cook over medium heat for 5 minutes. Add the fish sauce and pepper. Remove the cabbage. Arrange all vegetables, meat and broth into a large serving bowl. Serve hot with the Eggplant Sauce and steamed rice.

Serves 4
Preparation time: 25 minutes
Cooking time: 1 hour

3/4 lb (750 g) bone-in chicken pieces, cut into serving sections
3 chorizo de Bilbao or Chinese sausages, sliced
1/4 lb (125 g) ham, sliced
1 teaspoon salt
5 cups (1.25 liters) water
2 tablespoons oil
3 cloves garlic, crushed with the side of knife and minced
One 15-oz (420-g) can chickpeas, drained
1 potato, peeled, cubed and boiled
2 unripe saba bananas (or 1 small plantain or 2 unripe regular bananas), sliced
1/2 small head cabbage (about 1 lb/500 g), sliced
1 tablespoon fish sauce
1/4 teaspoon freshly ground black pepper

Eggplant Sauce (Makes about 1 cup/150 g)
1 Japanese or Italian eggplant or 1/2 globe eggplant (about 1/2 lb/250 g)
2 cloves garlic, crushed and minced
3 tablespoons Filipino cane vinegar (or cider vinegar diluted with water, page 13)
1/2 teaspoon salt
1/4 teaspoon freshly ground black pepper

Classic Filipino Chicken Pot Pie

Pastel de Pollo

In this scrumptious pot pie recipe, originally from Spain, chicken complements potatoes, carrots, green peas, and shiitake mushrooms. The earthy flavor is from the shiitake mushrooms—called "fragrant mushrooms" in Chinese—and either fresh or dried mushrooms can be used. The pies can be cooked in small pots or in ovenproof cups and baked in individual portions, which is what I usually do when I invite friends over. Whether served family style or individual servings, with or without steamed rice, this pie is simply irresistible. For a fancier presentation, you can create a decorative lattice on the crust.

If using dried shiitake mushrooms, soak them in warm water for 15 minutes. Remove and discard the mushroom stems and slice the mushroom caps.

Combine the soy sauce and lime juice in a mixing bowl. Add the chicken and marinate for 1 hour in the refrigerator.

In a saucepan, add the chicken, water, salt and pepper and cook over medium heat for 15 minutes. With a slotted spoon, remove the chicken and set aside. Reserve the broth.

Heat a skillet over medium heat and melt the butter. Add the chicken and Vienna sausages and sauté for 5 minutes. Remove from the skillet and set aside.

To the same skillet, add the reserved broth, potato, carrot, celery, and green peas and cook over medium heat for 15 minutes, or until cooked. Add the mushrooms, sautéed chicken, and Vienna sausage and cook for 5 minutes more. Transfer to a 9-inch (22-cm) deep-dish pie pan or four 7-ounce (200-ml) heatproof cups.

Pre-heat the oven to 375°F (190°C).

To make the pie crust, place the flour, cold water, oil, and salt in a mixing bowl and mix thoroughly to make a thick dough. Form the dough into a ball, if using a pie pan, or into 4 equal-size balls if using individual cups. On a floured surface, roll out the dough with a rolling pin into either one large circle, about 12 inches (30 cm) across, if using a pie pan; or, into four 3-inch (7.5 cm) circles, if using individual cups. Note: If you want to make a latticed upper crust, cut the dough into long strips and place them over the chicken mixture in alternating strips to form a lattice pattern, and seal the edges. To make a solid top crust, simply transfer the dough to the pie pan or cups and cover the chicken mixture. Seal the edges by pressing down with fingers. Cut off the excess dough around the edges with a knife. If using a solid crust, make slits on the dough to let off steam. Brush with the beaten egg.

Bake for 20 minutes or until golden brown. Serve hot with steamed rice.

Serves 4
Preparation time: 15 minutes + 1 hour marinating time
Cooking time: 1 hour

1/2 lb (250 g) boneless, skinless chicken breasts or thighs, diced
3 tablespoons soy sauce
3 tablespoons freshly squeezed lime juice
3 cups (750 ml) water
1 teaspoon salt
1/2 teaspoon freshly ground black pepper
1 tablespoon unsalted butter
One 5-oz (142-g) can Vienna sausage, sliced
1 potato, peeled and diced
1 carrot, peeled and diced
1 stalk celery, diced
1/2 cup (75 g) fresh or frozen green peas
5 fresh or dried shiitake mushrooms
1 egg, beaten

Pie Crust
1 cup (125 g) all-purpose flour
3 tablespoons cold water
3 tablespoons oil
1/2 teaspoon salt

chapter 5
seafood dishes

The Philippines is an archipelago of 7,107 islands with more than 21,000 miles (33,000 km) of shoreline. It has numerous tropical seas, rivers, and lakes. With geographic features like these, it means that fresh seafood is abundantly available and a Filipino staple. In fact, the waters around these islands contain more than 2,000 species of fish—such as grouper (*lapu-lapu*), sea bass (*apahap*), tuna, and mackerel—and that's just from the ocean!

Popular freshwater species include mullet (*banak*) and freshwater crabs. Commercial fishponds provide a constant supply of tilapia, mudfish, catfish, squid, prawns, and milkfish (*bangus*). The milkfish is the national fish of the Philippines and is widely exported in frozen, smoked, or canned form. With so much bounty from the seas and rivers, Filipinos have traditionally always eaten more seafood and reserved meat only for special occasions.

Local seafoods are preserved by either smoking (*tinapa*) or sun-drying (*daing*). A third method is to debone and marinate them in vinegar and garlic and then freeze them. Boneless preserved bangus from the province of Pangasinan has become popular all over the country.

Aside from being a main ingredient in several dishes, fish and shrimp are also fermented to make fish sauce (*patis*), anchovy sauce (*bagoong isda*) and shrimp paste (*bagoong alamang*). These indispensable seasonings provide a strong, pungent smell and a salty taste. If you are new to patis and bagoong, it may take some time to get accustomed to the taste, but they actually do make foods taste better—just as soy sauce enhances food in Chinese or Japanese cooking. Use them like you would use salt in your cooking or as a condiment or dip.

If the thought of handling fresh fish makes you squeamish you can have the fish scaled, cleaned, and trimmed by a fishmonger. Fish bought from a fishmonger tends to be fresher than fish from a supermarket.

Sautéed Squid   Guisadong Pusit

Squid is a popular ingredient in the Philippines and is an excellent source of protein. For this dish, tender squid is sautéed in a spicy and sweet tomato-based sauce to create a hearty meal. It's important not to overcook the squid as it not only toughens, but it loses its flavor and texture as well. I've provided instructions on how to clean a squid correctly.

Prepare fresh squid, if using, by following the steps below. Cut into rings and set aside.

   Heat a skillet over medium heat and add the oil. Add the garlic and sautè until lightly browned. Add the onion and sauté until translucent. Add the squid and sauté over medium heat for 3 minutes, or until cooked, while stirring frequently. The meat will turn opaque. Add the tomato, chili pepper, soy sauce, fish sauce, and sugar and simmer over medium heat for another 3 minutes. Season with the pepper. Serve hot with steamed rice.

Serves 4
Preparation time: 10 minutes +
   15 minutes to clean fresh squid
Cooking time: 10 minutes

2 lbs (1 kg) fresh or frozen squid
2 tablespoons oil
3 cloves garlic, crushed with the side of knife
1 onion, chopped
1 tomato, diced
1 finger-length green chili pepper, minced
1 tablespoon soy sauce
1 tablespoon fish sauce
$1/2$ teaspoon sugar
$1/4$ teaspoon freshly ground black pepper

How to Clean Fresh Squid

1 Wash the squid with cold water. Holding the body with one hand, grasp the head with your other hand and slightly twist and pull the tentacles and innards from the body. Trim the longest tentacles. Cut and discard the innards (the ink sac is inside the innards; it is edible and can be used for other dishes).

2 At the base of the tentacles just above the eyes, there is a bony piece of inedible cartilage which is the squid's beak. Squeeze the base of the tentacles to pop the beak out. Remove the beak and discard it.

3 The body, or tube portion, contains an inedible thin, clear cartilage that looks like a plastic sheet. Pull out the cartilage and discard. The outer skin of the squid is edible but if you wish to remove it, you can use your finger to peel it away easily. Wash the tube under cold running water.

Sautéed Marinated Clams

Estofadong Tulya

Serves 4
Preparation time: 15 minutes + 1 hour
  marinating time
Cooking time: 15 minutes

Clams are popular everywhere in the Philippines, where they are harvested along reefs or even farmed to provide grocery stores and restaurants with fresh clam meat. This delicious clam dish uses a vinegar marinade. The clams are then sautéed in soy sauce and brown sugar, creating a savory and sweet combination. It's a simple dish with only a few ingredients making it ideal for a quick weekday meal.

1 tablespoon oil
3 cloves garlic, crushed with the side of knife
1 onion, thinly sliced
1 lb (500 g) canned or fresh clam meat (from about 4 lbs/2 kg fresh soft-shelled clams)
1/2 cup (45 g) breadcrumbs
1/2 teaspoon salt
1 teaspoon brown sugar

Combine the Marinade ingredients in a mixing bowl. Add the clams and marinate for 1 hour.

Heat a skillet over medium heat and add the oil. Add the garlic and sauté until lightly browned. Add the onion and sauté until translucent.

Add the clams. Cook over medium heat for 5 minutes, or until tender. Add the breadcrumbs, salt and brown sugar and cook for 5 more minutes, stirring occasionally. Serve hot with steamed rice.

Marinade
3 tablespoons Filipino cane vinegar (or white vinegar or cider vinegar diluted with water, page 13)
1 teaspoon freshly ground black pepper
1 bay leaf

Fried Whole Fish with Eggs

Fried Whole Fish with Eggs

Sarsiadong Tilapia

Serves 4
Preparation time: 15 minutes
Cooking time: 20 minutes

2 lbs (1 kg) whole tilapia, snapper, or catfish, scaled, gutted and cleaned, or 1 1/2 lbs (750 g) fish fillets or steaks

1 teaspoon salt

3 tablespoons oil

3 cloves garlic, crushed with the side of knife

1 onion, chopped

1 bunch spinach (about 1/2 lb/250 g), destemmed and chopped

2 tomatoes, diced

1/2 teaspoon freshly ground black pepper

1 tablespoon water

3 eggs, beaten

This delicious Kapampangan dish calls for a whole tilapia that is crisp-fried and then topped with scrambled eggs, tomato and spinach. My husband loves this dish, so he normally does the cooking. He loves the fish crispy and brown. When the vegetable and egg mixture is poured over the fish it makes for a colorful presentation. Tilapia is a fish you can easily find at the grocery store or fish market and is a good source of protein that is low in calorie and fat content. Snapper or catfish are good alternatives but try to use a whole fish (rather than fillets or steaks) for a crispier and better texture.

Wash the fish thoroughly. Pat dry and rub the outside with the salt (if using fish fillets or steaks, reduce the amount of salt to 1/2 teaspoon).

Heat a large skillet over medium heat, and add 2 tablespoons of the oil. Add the fish and fry each side for 10 minutes or until lightly browned. If you're using fillets or steaks, the cooking time will be less (10 minutes per inch is a good general rule). While the fish is browning, begin cooking the eggs and vegetables, but remember to check back on the fish time and again so as to not burn it. The fish flesh will appear opaque and be flaky when done.

Heat a separate skillet over medium heat, and add the remaining 1 tablespoon of the oil. Add the garlic and sauté until lightly browned. Add the onion and sauté until translucent. Add the spinach, tomatoes, and black pepper and cook for 5 minutes. Add the water and eggs, and cook for 3 minutes, stirring frequently.

Transfer the crispy tilapia to a serving platter, and pour the scrambled egg and vegetable mixture over it. Serve hot with steamed rice.

Sauteéd Shrimp with Long Beans

Guisadong Sitaw

Serves 4
Preparation time: 5 minutes
Cooking time: 20 minutes

1 tablespoon oil

3 cloves garlic, crushed with the side of knife

1 onion, thinly sliced

1/2 lb (250 g) long beans or green beans, sliced into 2-in (5-cm) lengths

1 large tomato, diced

1 lb (500 g) fresh shrimp, shelled and deveined

1 tablespoon bottled sautéed shrimp paste (page 16) or more to taste

1/4 teaspoon freshly ground black pepper

When I was living in the Philippines, I could go out to my backyard and pick *sitaw*, or long beans, whenever I wanted to use them for this dish. These tasty beans, which can be substituted with regular green beans, make a wonderful backdrop for the sautéed shrimp and sautéed shrimp paste (bagoong) that give this dish its salty and robust flavor.

Heat a skillet over medium heat and add the oil. Add the garlic and sauté until lightly browned. Add the onion and sauté until translucent. Add the beans and tomato and sauté for 10 minutes or until the beans are tender. Add the shrimp and sauté for 5 minutes, stirring frequently.

Add the shrimp paste and pepper, and simmer over medium-low heat for about 5 minutes to settle the flavor. Taste and add another teaspoon or two of shrimp paste if desired. Serve hot with steamed rice.

Fried Marinated Fish

Daing na Bangus

The traditional method of preserving fish—salting and sun drying—is time-consuming and labor-intensive. By marinating the fish in vinegar with plenty of garlic overnight you'll get the same great taste without the time and labor. When I was in the Philippines, I especially enjoyed this dish when it was made with fresh milkfish caught in a nearby pond. Milkfish is traditionally used for this dish but rainbow trout, sea bass, or mackerel are good substitutes. This dish goes wonderfully well with Pickled Green Papaya (page 21) and a vinegar-based dip of your choice.

Combine the Marinade ingredients in a bowl and stir until the salt is dissolved. Open the fish like a book and place it skin-side up in a large casserole dish. Pour the Marinade over it and let marinate in the refrigerator overnight.

Heat a skillet over medium heat and add the oil. Fry the fish for about 15 minutes on each side or until brown. Serve hot with and hot steamed rice, Pickled Green Papaya (page 21) and Vinegar Garlic Sauce (page 20) or Vinegar and Sauteed Shrimp Paste Sauce (page 21).

Serves 4
Preparation time: 5 minutes + overnight marinating time
Cooking time: 30 minutes

2 lbs (1 kg) whole milkfish, rainbow trout, sea bass or mackerel, scaled, gutted and cleaned, or 1 1/2 lbs (750 g) fish fillets
3 tablespoons oil
Pickled Green Papaya (page 21)
Vinegar Garlic Sauce (page 20) or Vinegar and Sautéed Shrimp Paste Sauce (page 21), for dipping

Marinade
1 cup (250 ml) Filipino cane vinegar (or white vinegar or cider vinegar diluted with water, page 13)
5 cloves garlic, crushed with the side of knife
1 tablespoon salt
1 teaspoon freshly ground black pepper

Sweet and Sour Fish

Escabeche

To make this delicious dish, a whole fish—preferably a *lapu-lapu*, but any grouper will do—is marinated, fried, and simmered in a heavenly sweet-and-sour sauce. Bell peppers add color to the dish and enhance the flavor. Lapu-lapu is a red grouper indigenous to the Philippines and is also the name of the king of Mactan Island who valiantly fought and vanquished the Spanish explorer Ferdinand Magellan in 1521.

Combine the lime juice and salt in a small bowl and stir until the salt is dissolved. Place the fish in a large casserole dish and pour the salted lime juice over the fish. Let stand for 30 minutes.

Heat a skillet over medium heat, add 1 tablespoon of the oil and fry the fish for 10 minutes on each side, or until cooked. The fish should be flaky when done. Transfer to a serving platter and set aside.

Heat a skillet over medium heat, add 1 tablespoon of the oil and sauté the garlic until lightly browned. Add the onion and sauté until translucent. Add the ginger, bell pepper, and carrot and sauté for 3 minutes. Stir in the vinegar, water, soy sauce, sugar and banana ketchup. Bring to a boil, stir in the cornstarch mixture and simmer over medium-low heat until it thickens. Pour the sauce over the fish. Serve with steamed rice.

Serves 4
Preparation time: 10 minutes +
  30 minutes marinating time
Cooking time: 30 minutes

4 tablespoons freshly squeezed lime juice
1 tablespoon salt (use 1¹/₂ teaspoons if using fish steaks or fillets)
2 tablespoons oil
2 lbs (1 kg) whole fish, scaled, gutted, and cleaned, or 1¹/₂ lbs (750 g) fish steaks or fillets (grouper, red snapper, carp, cod, or bass)
3 cloves garlic, crushed with the side of knife
1 onion, sliced
One 2-in (5-cm) piece ginger, finely sliced
1 bell pepper, deseeded and finely sliced
1 carrot, peeled and finely sliced
3 tablespoons Filipino cane vinegar (or white vinegar or cider vinegar diluted with water, page 13)
4 tablespoons water
1 tablespoon soy sauce
3 tablespoons brown sugar
1 tablespoon banana ketchup
1 tablespoon cornstarch dissolved in 2 tablespoons water

Piquant Fish Stew

Paksiw na Isda

The city of Dagupan in Pangasinan organizes a yearly festival to celebrate their production of milkfish, and this Paksiw dish is one of the popular dishes served at the festival. In the old days, freshly caught fish were immediately soaked in vinegar to preserve them; this recipe evolved from this method of preserving fish. This is a slightly spicy version that I like to prepare for weekday meals (the leftovers keep well in the refrigerator). Any fresh fish will do, although milkfish and *galunggong*, a type of mackerel popular in the Philippines, are favorite choices.

Combine the water, vinegar, garlic, bitter gourd, if using, and ginger in a saucepan. Add the fish and bring to a boil. Reduce the heat to medium-low and add the fish sauce, salt and chili peppers. Simmer for about 20 minutes, or until cooked. Fish should flake easily with a fork. Serve hot with steamed rice.

Serves 4
Preparation time: 5 minutes
Cooking time: 20 minutes

1¹/₂ lbs (750 g) fish fillets (milkfish, rainbow trout, sea bass or mackerel)
1 cup (250 ml) water
2 cups (500 ml) Filipino cane vinegar (or white vinegar or cider vinegar diluted with water, page 13)
5 cloves garlic, crushed with the side of knife
1 bitter gourd (about 1 lb/500 g), cut in half lengthwise, deseeded and sliced into half-moons (optional)
One 2-in (5-cm) piece ginger, peeled and finely sliced
1 tablespoon fish sauce
1 teaspoon salt
3 finger-length green chili peppers

Stuffed Crabs   Rellenong Alimasag

Serves 4
Preparation time: 1 hour
Cooking time: 1 hour

This dish is time-consuming but the result is worth it. I find that some crabs don't have much meat, so I buy an extra crab or two to make sure the crabs I serve are nicely stuffed.

5 lbs (2.25 kg) fresh crabs (about 10 small fresh crabs or 5 medium ones)
8 cups (2 liters) water
1½ teaspoons salt
2 tablespoons oil
3 cloves garlic, crushed with the side of knife and minced
1 small onion, minced
1 small tomato, diced
2 potatoes, peeled and diced
1 teaspoon soy sauce
½ teaspoon freshly ground black pepper
1 egg, beaten
1 tablespoon cornstarch dissolved in 2 tablespoons water
1 tablespoon breadcrumbs
Sweet and Spicy Sauce (page 21) or banana ketchup

Wash the crabs thoroughly under running water. Bring the water and 1 teaspoon of the salt to a boil in a saucepan. Submerge the crabs and boil for 5 to 10 minutes. Take the crabs out and set aside.

To remove the crabmeat, break the crab legs and claws off with your fingers. Place the crab with their underside facing up on a cutting board. Use a small knife to pry up the end of the crab's "apron" (this is a small tab) and pull it off. Pry the hard shell off the body (you can use your hands to do this or a small knife inserted at the rear of the crab where the apron has been removed). With a small knife, scrape off the gills—a grayish white matter—and discard. Break the body in two to make it easier to remove the meat (you can do this with your hands or with kitchen shears). If the legs and/or claws look meaty, use kitchen shears to cut them in half and remove the meat. Discard the body cavity and legs after removing the meat. Set the crabmeat aside. Clean and reserve the outer shell of 8 of the small crabs or 4 or the medium-size crabs. Discard the remaining shells.

Add 1 tablespoon of the oil to a skillet over medium heat. Add the garlic and sauté until lightly browned. Add the onion and sauté until translucent. Add the tomato and potato and sauté for 10 minutes, or until soft. Add the crabmeat, soy sauce, remaining ½ teaspoon of salt and the pepper. Cook for another 5 minutes, stirring frequently. Remove from the heat and let the mixture cool to room temperature.

Fill each crab shell with the mixture, pressing lightly with a spoon. Brush egg over the mixture. Lightly drizzle the cornstarch mixture over the filling (use the back of a spoon to spread it around). Then sprinkle and lightly press the breadcrumbs on top of the cornstarch.

Add the remaining 1 tablespoon of the oil to a skillet over medium heat. Place the shells stuffing-side down and fry for about 15 minutes, or until lightly browned. Alternatively, bake in a preheated oven at 425°F (220°C) for 15 minutes stuffing side up. Serve with steamed rice and banana ketchup or Sweet and Spicy Sauce (page 21).

Filipino Ceviche

Kinilaw na Tanigue

Filipinos from the central Visayan islands are especially good at making *kinilaw*—a method of marinating raw seafood in vinegar and spices. Freshly caught fish are typically used, though the Ilocanos from the northern part of Luzon even prepare this dish using goat meat! Spanish mackerel is popular for this dish but any other fish or shrimp, oysters or squid will do just as nicely. Make sure that you use very fresh fish and serve the dish immediately. If you are concerned about the freshness of the fish, look for sashimi-grade tuna or salmon.

Pour the vinegar into a mixing bowl, add the fish and marinate for 1 hour. Drain. In a serving bowl, combine the calamansi juice, ginger, onion, chili, salt and pepper. Mix thoroughly. Add the fish. Chill in the refrigerator for 1 hour to allow the flavors to mingle. Serve immediately with hot steamed rice.

Serves 4
Preparation time: 10 minutes + 2 hours marinating time

1/2 cup (125 ml) Filipino cane vinegar (or white vinegar or cider vinegar diluted with water, page 13)
1 lb (500 g) Spanish mackerel, sea bass, tuna or salmon fillets, washed, skinned and cut into cubes
4 tablespoons freshly squeezed calamansi or lime juice
One 2-in (5-cm) piece ginger, peeled and thinly sliced
1/2 onion, thinly sliced
1 finger-length green chili pepper, thinly sliced
1/2 teaspoon salt
1/4 teaspoon freshly ground black pepper

chapter 6
vegetables

In the tropics, vegetables are abundant and nearly everyone has a garden in his or her backyard, though Filipinos are not known for their consumption of vegetable-only dishes. Sadly, vegetable dishes are often associated with a poor person's diet. Filipinos, however, love to mix vegetables with bits of pork or beef or slices of chicken or fish and add vegetables to soups and stews for extra color or flavor. Some common local vegetables are water spinach (*kangkong*), white gourd (*upo*), long beans (*sitaw*), eggplant (*talong*), moringa leaves (*malunggay*) and chayote (*sayote*). Tendrils or shoots of some vegetables (called *talbos*) are very popular as well. Young unripe papaya is also cooked like a vegetable.

The king of Filipino vegetables is probably the bitter gourd (*ampalaya*), a native of the tropics that is used in a wide variety of dishes in the Philippines. It has a bitter taste, as its name suggests, but it is rich in iron, betacarotene, and other nutrients that boost the body's immune system. Fresh bitter gourd is sometimes hard to find outside of the Philippines, but frozen, bottled, or canned varieties are available from Asian supermarkets or online grocery stores.

The prudent Ilocano people from the northern part of Luzon are particularly known for their love of vegetables. Their signature dish is Pinakbet, a mixed vegetable dish consisting of bitter gourd, eggplant, tomato, okra, long beans, and shrimp paste. Variations on this dish can be found in almost all regions of the country and each cook often seems to have his or her own version.

Western-style salads are seldom found on Filipino dining tables, but are served at restaurants. Filipino-style "salads"—served with almost every meal—are made with local vegetables that are either steamed or boiled and seasoned with a distinct Filipino dressing made of fish sauce, shrimp paste and calamansi lime. Pickled vegetables, like Pickled Green Papaya (page 21), are also very popular.

Pinakbet

Mixed Vegetables with Anchovy Sauce

In this healthy Ilocano dish, bitter gourd, eggplant, okra and long beans are simmered in a tasty fish sauce—though some Filipinos prefer sauteed shrimp paste as in the photograph above. I have tasted different versions of Pinakbet but no one makes it like the Ilocanos. My Ilocano friends, Vilma and Regina, always make impeccable Pinakbet, so I'm giving their recipe here. Ilocanos discovered long ago that stirring bitter gourd makes it even more bitter. Do not stir the bitter gourd while it is cooking, just let the steam cook the vegetables. If you have some fried pork rinds in your cupboard, use them as a topping.

Place the bitter gourd in the bottom of a large saucepan, and then add the ginger, long beans, onion, okra, tomato, eggplant and sauteed shrimp paste, if using. Pour the water and anchovy sauce into the saucepan and bring to a boil. Reduce the heat to medium and cover. Leave for 20 minutes or until vegetables are tender and cooked. Do not stir, but instead, shake the pan once or twice. Garnish with the crushed fried pork rinds, if using, and serve hot with steamed rice.

Serves 4
Preparation time: 10 minutes
Cooking time: 20 minutes

1 small bitter gourd (about $1/2$ lb/255 g), cut in half lengthwise, deseeded and sliced

One 2-in (5-cm) piece ginger, peeled and sliced

$1/4$ lb (125 g) long beans or green beans, trimmed and sliced into 2 in (5 cm)

1 onion, chopped

$1/4$ lb (125 g) fresh or frozen okra, trimmed

1 tomato, diced

1 Japanese or Italian eggplant or $1/2$ globe eggplant (about $1/2$ lb/250 g), cut in half lengthwise and sliced

$1/2$ cup (125 ml) water

3 tablespoons bottled anchovy sauce (page 12) or bottled sautéed shrimp paste (page 16)

One 3-oz (75-g) bag fried pork rinds (chicharon), crushed (optional)

Mung Bean and Spinach Stew

Guisadong Munggo

This dish is popular on Fridays, when Catholic Filipinos traditionally go without meat. Mung beans don't require pre-soaking but soaking them does make them more tender and allows them to cook more evenly. Filipinos always associate mung beans with *talbos ng kamote* (sweet potato tendrils) and *chicharon* (fried pork rinds) in this simple but tasty stew. If it's not Friday, or if you're not Catholic, including chicharon adds texture and taste to the dish. Pork rind is a versatile ingredient that can be eaten as a snack, with rice, or crumbled over a stew or soup. Once it gets wet it becomes soft and chewy.

Heat a skillet over medium heat, add the oil and sauté the garlic until lightly browned. Add the onion and sauté until translucent. Add the shrimp and cook for 3 minutes or until they become opaque. Remove from the heat and set aside.

Place the beans and water in a saucepan. Bring to a boil and cook over medium heat for about 20 minutes or until soft. Add the fish sauce, sautéed shrimp paste, and pepper. Add the sautéed shrimp, garlic, onion and simmer over medium-low heat until the beans are soft. Add more water if needed.

Add the spinach and simmer over low heat for 1 more minute. Before transferring to a serving dish add the chopped pork rind, if using. Top with the crushed fried pork rinds, if using, and serve hot with steamed rice.

Serves 4
Preparation time: 10 minutes
 + overnight soaking time
Cooking time: 30 minutes

1 tablespoon oil
3 cloves garlic, crushed with the side of a knife
1 onion, thinly sliced
1/4 lb (125g) fresh shrimp, shelled and deveined
1 cup (200 g) dried mung beans, soaked in water overnight and drained
2 cups (500 ml) water
2 tablespoons fish sauce
1 tablespoon bottled sautéed shrimp paste (page 16)
1/4 teaspoon freshly ground black pepper
1 bunch (about 1/2 lb/225 g) fresh spinach (or any other fresh leafy green vegetable), chopped
One 3-oz (75-g) bag fried pork rinds (chicharon), crushed (optional)

Braised Chayote with Shrimp

Guisadong Sayote

Green juicy chayote contrasts beautifully in color and texture with the savory shrimp used in this dish. Inexpensive chayote is common in the Philippines; it is native to Mexico, and is a member of the gourd family. The tropical Philippine climate makes chayote available throughout the year. This is another simple weekday dish that is simple to make and satisfying. If you can't find chayote then zucchini, green papaya, or summer squash make excellent substitutes.

Heat a skillet over medium heat, add the oil and sauté the garlic until lightly browned. Add the onion and sauté until translucent. Add the shrimp and sauté for 3 more minutes, or until the shrimp becomes opaque. Remove from the heat and set aside.

In a separate saucepan, bring 4 cups (1 liter) of the water to a boil. Add the chayote and cook over high heat for 15 minutes or until soft. Drain well and set aside.

To the skillet with the sautéed shrimp mixture, add the cooked chayote, the remaining 1/2 cup (125 ml) of water and the sautéed shrimp paste. Simmer over medium-low heat for 5 minutes. Add the salt and pepper. Serve hot with steamed rice.

Serves 4
Preparation time: 10 minutes
Cooking time: 15 minutes

1 tablespoon oil
5 cloves garlic, crushed with the side of a knife
1 onion, diced
1/4 lb (125 g) fresh shrimp, shelled and deveined
41/2 cups (1 liter plus 125 ml) water
1 chayote (about 11/2 lbs/750 g), peeled, deseeded and thinly sliced
1 tablespoon bottled sautéed shrimp paste (page 16)
1/4 teaspoon salt
1/2 teaspoon freshly ground black pepper

Banana Blossom with Shrimp

Kilawing Puso ng Saging

The banana blossom is reddish-purple on the outside and heart-shaped, which is why it is also known as a "banana heart." Soaking the blossom in salted water makes the slices less sticky and prevents discoloration as well. Canned banana blossom or fresh artichoke or zucchini blossoms make acceptable substitutes.

Prepare the fresh banana blossom, if using, by following the steps below. Canned banana blossom needs no soaking. Marinate the fresh or canned blossom in the vinegar for 1 hour. Reserve the vinegar.

Twist and pull the heads off the shrimp. Set the shrimp aside. Mash the shells and heads in a mortar. Pour the 1/2 cup (125 ml) of water into the mortar. Discard the shells and head and reserve the liquid.

Heat a skillet over medium heat and add the oil. Add the garlic and sauté until lightly browned. Add the onion and sauté until translucent. Add the shrimp and sauté for 3 minutes. Add the banana blossom, the reserved vinegar and the shrimp liquid, and simmer over medium-low heat for 20 minutes, or until soft and tender. Add the pepper, sautéed shrimp paste, and sugar. Simmer for 5 more minutes. Serve hot with steamed rice.

Serves 4
Preparation time: 25 minutes + marinating time
Cooking time: 30 minutes

- 1 banana blossom, fresh or canned
- 4 cups (1 liter) water plus 1 tablespoon salt
- 1 cup (250 ml) Filipino cane vinegar (page 13)
- 1/4 lb (125 g) fresh shrimp with heads on, shelled and deveined
- 1/2 cup (125 ml) water
- 1 tablespoon oil
- 5 cloves garlic, crushed
- 1 onion, finely sliced
- 1/4 teaspoon freshly ground black pepper
- 1 tablespoon bottled sautéed shrimp paste (page 16)
- 1/2 teaspoon brown sugar

How to Prepare Fresh Banana Blossom

1 Remove and discard the dark outer layers of the blossom to expose the lighter inner layers. Cut off and discard the top part of the blossom.

2 Slice the remaining part into thin pieces.

3 Soak the slices in the 4 cups (1 liter) of salted water for at least 2 hours. Remove the slices and drain them; discard the salted water.

Stuffed Eggplant

Rellenong Talong

Filipino eggplants, or *talong,* are perfect for stuffing. Similar in size to Japanese eggplants, these purple-skinned eggplants are just the right size to accommodate a layer of cooked ground meat, providing a wonderful texture and taste to the meat mixture. After the meat is stuffed into the eggplant, it's then dipped in egg and fried or baked.

Pierce the eggplant(s) with a fork, place in a large pot of boiling water, and cook for about 10 minutes or until just tender (the larger globe eggplant will take longer to become tender). Holding the eggplants by their stalks, slice them lengthwise to open them like a book—do not slice all the way through—leaving the stalks intact. Place the eggplant(s) on a clean surface and flatten with a pestle or a back of a large spoon. Set aside.

Heat a large skillet over medium heat, and add 1 tablespoon of the oil. Add the garlic and sauté until lightly browned. Add the onion and tomato, and sauté for 3 minutes. Add the beef and sauté for 5 minutes. Add the salt, pepper, and sugar, and stir to combine. Remove the meat mixture from the skillet and divide into four portions. Set aside.

Beat the eggs in a large bowl. Submerge each eggplant in the egg, and place cut-side up on a large plate or a clean flat surface. Top each eggplant with one portion of the meat mixture and spread it evenly, pressing firmly. Pour the remaining egg over the stuffed eggplants.

To the same large skillet, add the remaining 2 tablespoons of oil and set over medium heat. Fry the stuffed eggplants, stuffed-side up first, until browned. Fry the other side. If baking, place the eggplants, stuffed-side up, on a sheet pan and bake in a pre-heated 400°F (200°C) oven for 30 minutes. Serve hot with banana ketchup and steamed rice.

Serves 4
Preparation time: 15 minutes
Cooking time: 30 minutes

4 Japanese or Italian eggplants or 1 large American "globe" eggplant
3 tablespoons oil
3 cloves garlic, crushed with the side of a knife and minced
1 onion, minced
1 tomato, minced
1 1/2 lbs (750 g) ground beef
1 teaspoon salt
1/2 teaspoon freshly ground black pepper
1 teaspoon sugar
4 eggs

Sautéed Corn with Shrimp

Guisadong Mais

The Spanish colonizers introduced corn to the region from Mexico and it is now the Philippines' second leading staple after rice. It is often planted in areas unsuitable for growing rice and has become a rice substitute for many Filipinos. In this dish, the natural sweetness of corn is added to juicy fresh shrimp and tender spinach. Remember not to overcook the shrimp or they will lose much of their sweetness.

Heat a skillet over medium heat, add the oil and garlic and sauté until lightly browned. Add the onion until translucent. Add the shrimp, corn, and spinach, and sauté for 10 minutes.

Add the fish sauce, salt and pepper. Sauté over medium-low heat for 5 more minutes. Serve hot with steamed rice.

Serves 4
Preparation time: 15 minutes
Cooking time: 15 minutes

1 tablespoon oil
3 cloves garlic, crushed with the side of a knife and minced
1 onion, diced
1/4 lb (125 g) fresh shrimp, shelled and deveined
3 cups (350 g) corn kernels (fresh or frozen)
1/4 lb (125 g) spinach, trimmed and chopped
1 tablespoon fish sauce
1/4 teaspoon salt
1 teaspoon freshly ground black pepper

Filipino Spinach and Egg Salad

Ensaladang Kangkong

Serves 4
Preparation time: 10 minutes
Cooking time: 15 minutes

1 lb (500 g) water spinach (or regular
   spinach or sweet potato greens)
1 tomato, cut into bite-size pieces
1 onion, thinly sliced
1 potato, peeled, diced and boiled
3 hard-boiled eggs, sliced
Vinegar and Sautéed Shrimp Paste Sauce
   (page 21), for garnish

This salad is traditionally made with water spinach, or *kangkong*, which is available anywhere in the Philippines and is sold worldwide in Vietnamese or Thai markets. Regular spinach or *talbos ng kamote* (sweet potato greens) can be substituted instead. Serve with Vinegar and Sautéed Shrimp Paste Sauce (page 21).

Wash the water spinach well and remove the leaves. Cut the stems into short lengths.

   Boil the stems for 5 minutes. Add the leaves and boil for another 3 minutes. Rinse with cold water and drain well.

   Combine the water spinach, tomato, onion, and potato in a mixing bowl. Mix thoroughly.

   Place the vegetables on a large serving platter or divide them among four individual salad bowls. Garnish with the egg slices. Drizzle Vinegar and Sautéed Shrimp Paste Sauce (page 21).

chapter 7
rice and noodle dishes

Rice is so important to the Filipino diet that no meal is ever complete without it. A typical day may start with a simple meal of steamed rice and a tasty sun-dried salted fish, called *tuyo*, dipped in vinegar with sliced tomato on the side. Filipinos appreciate such simple delicacies accompanied by a heaping mound of white steamed rice, or kanin. Hot, fluffy rice goes well with just about any dish and is eaten at any time— breakfast, lunch, dinner and even *merienda* (snack). For a Filipino, a simple *sarsa* (sauce) or *sabaw* (soup) can turn *kanin* (steamed rice) into a full meal.

Traditions relating to rice abound in the Philippines—throwing rice confetti at a newlywed couple brings them good fortune; the kitchen rice container must be full at the end of the year to welcome in a prosperous new year; and when moving into a new home, rice should be the first item brought into the house. Aside from being the star of any meal, rice is used to make wine, flour, vinegar and noodles.

Noodle dishes, either stir-fried or added to soup, are an outstanding contribution from Chinese immigrants. Locally known as *pancit*, noodle dishes are served on birthdays to wish the celebrant a long and healthy life, while noodles in a broth are given to a sick child as a nutritious home remedy. The word pancit is a play on the Hokkien Chinese word *pian i sit*, which means "rushed" or "hurried"—a fitting description for the quick and easy noodle recipes in this chapter.

There are many kinds of noodles available in the Philippines but the one most associated with birthday celebrations, or any occasion for that matter, is rice vermicelli, or *bihon*, which is great for Fried Rice Noodles (page 93). And because pancit dishes—whether stir-fried or soup-based—include a panoply of ingredients from seafood, meat to vegetables, they also make nourishing main dishes to hot steamed rice.

Cuban Rice with Ground Beef

Arroz a la Cubana

This "Cuban-style" rice is originally a Latin American dish found in most of Spain's former colonies, including the Philippines. It is simple and inexpensive to make—steamed rice, fried egg, fried bananas and sautèed beef are served together on a platter, or separately for diners to combine as they please. The sweet smell of this dish comes from the bananas.

Serves 4
Preparation time: 15 minutes
Cooking time: 30 minutes

4 tablespoons oil
5 cloves garlic, crushed with the side of a knife and minced
1 onion, minced
1 lb (500 g) ground beef (or pork)
1 potato, peeled and diced
1/3 cup (40 g) fresh or frozen green peas
3 tablespoons raisins
1 tablespoon soy sauce
1 teaspoon salt
1/4 teaspoon freshly ground black pepper
4 unripe saba bananas (or 2 plantains or 4 unripe regular bananas), cut in half lengthwise
4 eggs
4 cups (720 g) cooked rice

Heat a skillet over medium heat and add 1 tablespoon of the oil. Add the garlic and sauté until lightly browned. Add the onion and sauté until translucent. Add the ground beef and cook over medium heat for 5 minutes, or until cooked, stirring frequently. Transfer the meat to a bowl and set aside.

To the same skillet over medium heat, add another 1 tablespoon of the oil. Add the potato and sauté for 10 minutes. When cooked, add the meat mixture, green peas, raisins, soy sauce, salt and pepper and cook for 5 more minutes. Spoon the meat mixture onto a serving platter and cover with foil to keep warm.

To the same skillet over medium heat, add 1 tablespoon of the oil and fry the bananas on each side for 5 minutes or until lightly browned. Add the bananas to the platter with the meat mixture and cover again with the foil.

To the same skillet over medium heat, add the remaining 1 tablespoon of oil and fry the eggs, sunny side up. Set aside.

Arrange the hot steamed rice, fried bananas, beef, and fried eggs on a large platter or serve individually. Serve hot with banana ketchup.

Cuban Rice with Ground Beef

Kapampangan Paella
Bringhe

Kapampangan Paella, locally known as *Bringhe*, is similar to Spanish Paella. However, glutinous sweet rice and turmeric are used instead of regular rice and saffron. The Kapampangan version uses coconut milk and is often cooked in banana leaves for an aroma that is sure to make guests hungry. Bringhe is a very popular dish for parties.

Serves 4 to 6
Preparation time: 15 minutes + 1 hour soaking time
Cooking time: 40 minutes

2 tablespoons oil
3 cloves garlic, crushed with the side of a knife and minced
1 onion, finely chopped
1 lb (500 g) boneless, skinless chicken breasts or thighs, cut into bite-size pieces
3 cups (600 g) uncooked glutinous rice, washed, soaked in water for at least 1 hour and drained
1 bell pepper, deseeded and sliced
One 13 1/2-oz (400-ml) can coconut milk
3 chorizo de Bilbao or Chinese dry sausages, thinly sliced
2 cups (500 ml) water
1 tablespoon ground turmeric
1 teaspoon salt
1/4 cup (50 g) raisins
1/2 teaspoon freshly ground black pepper
2 hard-boiled eggs, peeled and cut into wedges

Heat a skillet over medium heat and add 1 tablespoon of the oil. Add the garlic and sauté until lightly browned. Add the onion and sauté until translucent. Remove from the heat and set aside.

To a large skillet or sauté pan with a lid, add the remaining 1 tablespoon of oil and sauté the chicken over medium-high heat for about 5 minutes. Add the rice and sauté for about 3 minutes.

Add the bell pepper, coconut milk, sausage, water, turmeric and salt, and mix well. Bring to a boil. Then reduce the heat to medium-low heat and cover. Simmer for about 20 minutes or until the rice is cooked. Add the raisins and sautéed garlic and onion. Increase the heat to medium and cook for 5 minutes, stirring frequently. Add the black pepper and stir to combine. Transfer the rice to a serving platter and garnish with the eggs. Serve hot.

Filipino-Style Seafood Paella

Serves 4
Preparation time: 20 minutes
Cooking time: 45 minutes

Along with Kapampangan Paella (page 89), this version of paella is extremely popular and considered a typically Filipino dish despite its Spanish origins. This version is thought of as a rich person's paella since relatively expensive ingredients are used. This elegant and impressive meal is actually quite simple to make once you have prepared the ingredients. Many people love to serve this brightly colored paella at Christmas.

Add a bit of water to a pot and steam or boil the mussels over medium to high heat for about 5 minutes, or until the shells open. Discard any mussels that are not open. Set aside.

Add 1 tablespoon of the olive oil to a large skillet over medium heat. Add the shrimp and squid, and sauté for 3 minutes, or until cooked. Remove the shrimp and squid from the pan and set aside.

To the same skillet over medium heat, add 1 tablespoon of the oil. Add the garlic and sauté until lightly browned. Add the onion and sauté until translucent. Remove the garlic and onion from the pan and set aside.

Add the remaining 1 tablespoon of oil to the same large skillet over medium-high heat and sauté the rice for about 5 minutes. Add the water and bring to a boil. Reduce the heat to low and add the ginger, tomato, tomato sauce, paprika, salt and fish sauce. Add the sautéed garlic and onion. Mix thoroughly. Cover with a lid or aluminum foil and simmer over low heat for 20 minutes, or until the rice is cooked. Add the pepper and stir to combine.

Place the rice on a serving platter and top with the olives, shrimp, mussels and squid. Garnish with slices of lime. Serve hot.

12 fresh mussels in their shells, cleaned

3 tablespoons olive oil

1/2 lb (250 g) fresh shrimp with shells on

1/4 lb (125 g) fresh squid, cleaned and cut into rings (instructions on how to clean fresh squid on page 70) or frozen squid, defrosted and cut into rings

5 cloves garlic, crushed with the side of a knife and minced

1 onion, finely chopped

3 cups uncooked long-grain white rice, washed and drained

3 cups (750 ml) water

One 2-in (5-cm) piece ginger, peeled and thinly sliced

1 tomato, diced

One 8-oz (227-g) can tomato sauce

1 tablespoon paprika

1 teaspoon salt

1 tablespoon fish sauce

1/2 teaspoon freshly ground black pepper

1 cup (150 g) olives, pitted and sliced

3 limes, cut into segments, to garnish

Fried Rice with Egg Sinangag

Serves 4
Preparation time: 10 minutes
Cooking time: 15 minutes

Fried rice is a staple in all Asian countries where rice is eaten daily. It is the perfect way to use up cold leftover rice and other leftover ingredients. The Filipino version known as Sinangag, commonly eaten as a breakfast dish, is often accompanied with Filipino sausages (*longganisa*), hotdogs or Traditional Tocino Bacon (page 50). It is a starchy meal and a bit garlicky but everyone in the Philippines eats something substantial in the morning for energy and stamina. Warm, freshly cooked rice doesn't fry well. If you don't have any leftover rice, cook the rice and then chill it in the refrigerator before frying it.

2 tablespoons oil
5 cloves garlic, crushed with the side of a knife and minced
1 onion, minced
4 cups (750 g) cooked (and cooled) long-grain rice, grains gently separated with a fork or your fingers
3 eggs, lightly beaten
1 tablespoon soy sauce
1/2 teaspoon salt
1/4 teaspoon freshly ground black pepper
2 tablespoons Crispy Fried Garlic (page 23), to garnish (optional)
3 green onions (scallions), thinly sliced, green parts only, to garnish (optional)

Add 1 tablespoon of the oil to a skillet or wok over medium heat and sauté the garlic until lightly browned. Add the onion and sauté until translucent. Add the remaining 1 tablespoon of oil and increase the heat to high just before adding the rice. Stir-fry for 5 minutes, stirring constantly.

Pour the eggs over the rice and quickly stir-fry for 3 minutes, stirring vigorously.

Add the soy sauce, salt and pepper. Cook over medium to high heat for 5 minutes or until the rice becomes evenly browned. Garnish with Crispy Fried Garlic or green onions, if using. Serve hot.

Rice Porridge with Chicken

Arroz Caldo

Depending on the region, this porridge may be called Goto, Pospas, Lugaw, or Arroz Caldo (meaning "hot rice" in Spanish). This is actually a light, warm and nutritious Chinese congee adopted by the Spanish settlers. Traditionally, it is served to the elderly, the ill and toddlers because it's fortifying and easy to the digest. This version calls for Crispy Fried Garlic (page 23) on top—use a spoonful and you'll be amazed at the resulting taste!

Heat a skillet over medium heat and add 1 tablespoon of the oil. Add the 3 cloves of garlic and sauté until lightly browned. Rub the chicken with the salt and add to the skillet. Sauté for 15 minutes, or until lightly browned. Add the ginger and cook 1 more minute while stirring occasionally. Remove from the heat and set aside.

Add the uncooked rice and water to a stockpot and bring to a boil. Reduce the heat to low and add the sautéed garlic cloves, chicken and ginger mixture, Add the fish sauce. Cover and simmer over low heat for about 30 minutes or until the rice and chicken are cooked. If the rice gets too thick, add a little water.

Ladle the porridge into individual serving bowls. Squeeze some fresh lime juice over top and garnish with the green onion, Crispy Fried Garlic, and lime segments. Serve with soy sauce and fish sauce on the side.

Serves 4 to 6
Preparation time: 5 minutes
Cooking time: 1 hour

1 tablespoon oil
3 cloves garlic, crushed with the side of a knife
2 lbs (1 kg) bone-in chicken breasts, thighs or drumsticks, cut into pieces
1 teaspoon salt
One 2-in (5-cm) piece fresh ginger, peeled and finely sliced
2 cups (400 g) uncooked rice, washed and drained
7 cups (1.75 liters) water
3 tablespoons fish sauce
4 green onions (scallions), thinly sliced
5 fresh calamansi or regular limes, cut into segments
4 tablespoons Crispy Fried Garlic (page 23)
Soy sauce and fish sauce, to serve

Fried Rice Noodles

Bihon Guisado

When Filipinos think of noodles they think of the ubiquitous Bihon Guisado. Noodles symbolize longevity and good health, so this dish is a must-have on birthdays and special occasions. Chinese egg noodles also work well with this recipe.

Soak the rice vermicelli (*bihon*) in warm water for 5 minutes, drain and cut into desired length. Set aside.

Bring the water to a boil in a large saucepan. Add the chicken and salt and cook over high heat for 5 minutes or until cooked. Remove the chicken from the pan and set the broth aside (do not discard the broth). Tear the meat off the bones using two forks — one to hold the bone in place and one to tear the meat off the bone. Set the meat aside. Discard the bones.

Heat a large skillet over medium heat, add the oil and sauté the garlic until lightly browned. Add the onion and sauté until translucent. Add the shrimp, carrot, snow peas and celery and sauté for 5 minutes. Increase the heat to medium-high, add the cabbage, soy sauce, chicken and pepper, and sauté for 5 minutes. Add $1/2$ cup of the reserved chicken broth and the drained rice vermicelli and stir fry for 3–5 minutes. Add more of the reserved broth if rice vermicelli is too dry, stirring frequently. Transfer to a serving plate and serve hot with the calamansi or regular limes.

Serves 4
Preparation time: 15 minutes
+ 10 minutes soaking time
Cooking time: 35 minutes

8 oz (225 g) rice vermicelli
3 cups (725 ml) water
1 bone-in chicken thigh
$1/2$ tablespoon salt
2 tablespoons oil
4 cloves garlic, crushed and minced
1 onion, thinly sliced
$1/4$ lb (125 g) fresh shrimp, shelled and deveined
1 carrot, peeled and cut thinly
$1/4$ lb (125 g) snow peas, trimmed
1 large stalk celery, thinly sliced
2 cups (200 g) thinly sliced cabbage
1 tablespoon soy sauce
$1/2$ teaspoon freshly ground black pepper
4 calamansi or regular limes, quartered

Noodles with Shrimp and Tofu

Pancit Luglug

Initially, this dish might be confused with spaghetti, but it's really a unique dish that is bright orange in color and has the distinct aroma of cooked shrimp. This impressive dish—known as Pancit Luglug or Pancit Palabok depending on the region in which it is made—uses cornstarch noodles. When cooked, these noodles don't last long so they need to be consumed the day they are prepared. Dried rice vermicelli may be used in place of cornstarch noodles.

Noodles with Shrimp and Tofu

Serves 4
Preparation time: 15 minutes
Cooking time: 1 hour 30 minutes

1/2 lb (250 g) fresh shrimp, preferably with heads and tails on
2 tablespoons oil
3 cloves garlic, crushed with the side of a knife and minced
1 onion, minced
3 cups (750 ml) water
1/2 cup (75 g) diced pork shoulder or loin
One 3 1/2-oz (100-g) package deep-fried pressed tofu (tokwa), diced

1 teaspoon salt
1/2 cup (125 ml) annatto water (page 19) (optional)
2 tablespoons fish sauce
2 tablespoons cornstarch
8 cups (2 liters) water (for boiling noodles)
16 oz (500 g) cornstarch noodles (or rice vermicelli)
2 hard-boiled eggs, cut into wedges
2 green onions (scallions), thinly sliced (green part only)
4 limes, quartered
One 3-oz (75-g) bag fried pork rinds (chicharon), crushed (optional)

Twist and pull the heads off the shrimp. Shell and devein but leave the tails on. Set the cleaned shrimp tails aside. Mash the shrimp heads in a mortar or bowl. Pour the 3 cups (750 ml) of water, a little at time, while pressing the heads and shells against the side of the mortar or bowl with the back of a wooden spoon. Strain the shrimp liquid and set aside. Discard the mashed heads.

Heat a skillet over medium heat and add 1 tablespoon of the oil. Add the garlic and sauté until lightly browned. Add the onion and sauté until translucent. Transfer the garlic and onion to a bowl and set aside.

To the same skillet, over medium heat, add the remaining 1 tablespoon of the oil and sauté the diced pork for 5 minutes. Add the shrimp and tofu and sauté for 5 minutes. Add the salt and the sautéed garlic and onion. Stir to combine and set aside.

To make the shrimp sauce, combine the reserved shrimp liquid, annatto water, if using, fish sauce, and cornstarch in a saucepan. Simmer over medium-low heat for 10 minutes until the mixture thickens, stirring frequently to make sure the cornstarch is dissolved. Set aside.

Bring 8 cups (2 liters) of water to a boil in a large saucepan. Add the noodles and cook according to package instructions or until soft (about 7 minutes). Lightly rinse with cold running water to keep the noodles from sticking together. Drain well and transfer the noodles to a serving platter.

To serve, pour the shrimp sauce over the noodles and top with the pork mixture, hard-boiled eggs, and green onion. Squeeze some lime juice over the noodle mixture and sprinkle crushed fried pork rind. Garnish with lime quarters and serve hot.

Sautéed Bean Thread Noodles

Sotanghon Guisado

Celebrations call for this special dish of mung bean thread noodles, which have a smooth and delicate texture and are more expensive than other noodles. Also known as "cellophane noodles," these white noodles (*sotanghon* in Filipino), turn transparent when cooked (unlike rice vermicelli which keeps its white color). The flavor of this dish is brightened by the rich aroma of shiitake mushrooms, the crunch of snow peas, and a few drops of pungent fish sauce.

Serves 4
Preparation time: 15 minutes +15 minutes soaking time
Cooking time: 30 minutes

One 7-oz (220-g) package bean thread (cellophane) noodles
5 shiitake mushrooms (fresh or dried)
2 tablespoons oil
4 cloves garlic, crushed with the side of a knife
1 onion, finely sliced
1 carrot, peeled and cut into thin matchsticks
1 bone-in chicken thigh
1 1/4 teaspoons salt
3 cups (750 ml) water
1/4 lb (125 g) snow peas, trimmed
1 tablespoon fish sauce
1/4 teaspoon freshly ground black pepper
3 green onions (scallions), thinly sliced

Soak the noodles in a bowl of warm water for 15 minutes to soften, then drain well. (The noodles do not need to be completely soft.) Set aside.

If using dried shiitake mushrooms, soak them in warm water for 15 minutes. Remove and discard the mushroom stems and thinly slice the mushroom caps.

Heat a skillet over medium heat add the oil. Add the garlic and sauté until lightly browned. Add the onion and sauté until translucent. Add the carrot and sauté over medium heat for 10 minutes, stirring frequently. Remove from the heat and set aside.

Place the chicken, 1 teaspoon of the salt and the water in a saucepan and bring to a boil over high heat. Cook for 10 minutes. Remove the chicken from the pan and reserve the broth. Tear the meat off the bones using two forks—one to hold the bone in place and one to tear the meat off the bone. Set the meat aside. Discard the bones.

To the skillet with the sautéed carrot mixture, add the noodles, mushrooms, snow peas, fish sauce, black pepper chicken, reserved broth the remaining 1/4 teaspoon of the salt. Cook over medium heat for 5 minutes or until the noodles are soft. If the noodles get too dry, add a little water. Divide among 4 plates and garnish with the green onion. Serve immediately.

chapter 8
desserts and beverages

For a Filipino, the best time to have a dessert is anytime—between meals, during meals, and after meals. Filipinos are notoriously fond of sweets and have created some amazing *panghimugas* (desserts) to satisfy their sugar cravings. The most popular dessert on the islands is Halo-halo, a combination of sweet beans, fruits, shaved ice, toasted rice, milk, flan, and purple yam pudding. This is a classic summertime favorite. Other favorite desserts include Sweet Banana and Jackfruit Rolls (page 102), Toasted Butter Cookies (page 100), Sweet Purple Yam Pudding (page 99), and Filipino Leche Flan (page 108)—a rich custard with a layer of caramelized sugar on top.

Fruits such as pineapple, mango, banana, jackfruit, watermelon, guava, and papaya are used to make colorful additions to desserts. Coconut is a key ingredient in countless numbers of desserts—rich coconut milk is used to prepare Sweet Coconut Milk Delight (page 98) and fried coconut milk, or *latik*, makes a delicious topping for Sweet Rice Cakes with Fried Coconut Topping (page 100). Grated coconut garnishes the Coconut Sponge Cakes (page 103).

The cacao tree is native to the tropical Amazon forests and was brought to the Philippines by Spanish colonialists. Centuries later, the Filipinos have grown to love the chocolate that is made from the cacao fruit. Chocolate bars are used to make Chocolate Rice Porridge (page 98), a favorite of young and old Filipinos alike.

Like other tropical countries, the Philippines has a wide selection of *palamig* (cold drinks) to beat the heat. Street vendors sell the ever popular Iced Tapioca Pearl and Jelly Drink (page 106) on every corner.

Hot drinks make their appearance during the colder Christmas season, when Filipino Hot Chocolate (page 105) and Healthy Ginger Tea (page 107), soothe the throat and warm the body.

Champorado
Chocolate Rice Porridge

The Philippines has been growing cacao trees and creating chocolate treats ever since the Spanish brought the trees over in the seventeenth century. While Mexican *champurrado* is a thick chocolate drink, the Filipino version is a sweet dish of sticky rice and cocoa. Filipino children love to have this for breakfast and afternoon snacks. Grown-ups like to have it with salted fish (*tuyo*). Champorado is best served hot.

Serves 4
Preparation time: 5 minutes +
    30 minutes soaking time
Cooking time: 30 minutes

2 1/2 cups (750 ml) water
1 cup (200 g) uncooked glutinous
    rice, washed, soaked for at least 30
    minutes, and drained
3 1/2 oz (100 g) unsweetened chocolate
    or 1 cup (85 g) cocoa powder
1/2 cup (100 g) brown sugar
1/2 cup (125 ml) milk

Place water and glutinous rice in a saucepan and bring to a boil. Reduce the heat to the lowest setting. Cover and cook for 25 minutes more.

Add the chocolate or cocoa powder and sugar and stir over low heat. Mix well. If it gets too thick, add a little of the milk. Ladle the rice into bowls and serve with swirls of milk on top. Serve hot.

Sweet Coconut Milk Delight
Ginataang Bilo-bilo

A *ginataan* dish uses coconut milk (*gata*). This *ginataan* dessert contains jackfruit, sweet potato, tapioca pearls, and *bilo-bilo* (glutinous rice balls), simmered in sweet coconut milk. This traditional dish is a wonderful family dessert, ideal for a rainy afternoon. Serve it warm or chilled.

To make the rice balls, combine the rice flour with the 4 tablespoons of water in a bowl. Mix well and form into small balls, about 1/2 inch (1.25 cm) in diameter. Pour 8 cups (2 liters) of water into a pot and bring to a boil. Drop the balls in the boiling water and cook for 5 minutes, or until they float. Remove the rice balls and set aside.

Boil the tapioca pearls in the same pot over medium heat until soft and translucent. Drain and set aside.

In a saucepan, combine 2 cups (500 ml) of the coconut milk and the 2 cups (500 ml) of water and bring to a boil. Add sweet potato, and cook over medium heat for 15 minutes. Add the tapioca, sugar and rice balls, and cook for 10 minutes.

Add the jackfruit and banana and cook for 5 minutes until everything is tender. Add the remaining 1/2 cup (125 ml) of the coconut milk and bring to a boil. Reduce heat to low and simmer for 3 minutes more. Ladle onto individual bowls and serve warm or chilled.

Serves 4
Preparation time: 30 minutes
Cooking time: 30 minutes

1 cup (150 g) glutinous rice flour
4 tablespoons water (for rice
    balls)
8 cups (2 liters) water (for boiling)
1/2 cup (50g) dried tapioca pearls
2 1/2 cups (625 ml) coconut milk
2 cups (500 ml) water
2 1/2 cups (250 g) peeled and
    cubed sweet potato
1 cup (100 g) sugar
5 bulbs fresh or canned jackfruit,
    cut into strips
3 ripe saba bananas (or 3 regular
    bananas), sliced into rounds

Sweet Purple Yam Pudding

Ube Halaya

Ube, or purple yam, is a root crop that grows all over the country. It makes a colorful ingredient in a variety of desserts, such as ice cream, cakes and pastries. This pudding—made from purple yam powder that is readily available in groceries—is perfect by itself, but also makes a beautiful topping for Halo-halo (page 104).

Place the yam powder and milk in a saucepan and mix thoroughly. Add the sugar, egg and butter and simmer over low heat for about 1 hour. Stir constantly using a wooden spoon until the mixture thickens and becomes elastic.

Place the mixture in lightly greased containers with lid and let cool to room temperature. Do not cover while still hot. When cooled, cover and chill in the refrigerator for about 3 hours. Serve chilled in individual bowls.

Serves 4 to 6
Cooking time: 1 hour +
  3 hours chilling time

$3/_4$ cup (115 g) purple yam powder
$1^1/_2$ cups (375 ml) milk
$^1/_2$ cup (100 g) sugar
1 egg, beaten
1 teaspoon unsalted butter

Sweet Rice Cakes with Fried Coconut Topping

Biko Kalabasa

There are many variations on this traditional Kapampangan dessert and this version uses *latik,* or fried coconut milk solids, as a topping. Latik is made by reducing coconut milk to solids through boiling and then the solids are fried in their own oil, resulting in brown and nutty caramelized coconut bits. This delicious rice dessert is labor-intensive but the combination of latik, squash and glutinous rice tastes heavenly.

Serves 4 to 6
Preparation time: 10 minutes + 3 hours soaking time
Cooking time: 1 hour 30 minutes

3 cups (600 g) uncooked glutinous rice, washed, soaked for 3 hours and drained
3 cans coconut milk (13 1/2 oz/400 ml each)
1 lb (500 g) acorn squash, peeled, deseeded, and sliced to yield 4 cups (400 g)
3 cups (600 g) dark brown sugar
1 tablespoon unsalted butter, melted

Place the glutinous rice and 1 can of the coconut milk in a saucepan. Bring to a boil and reduce the heat to the lowest setting. Cook for 20 minutes and turn off the heat. Leave for another 15 minutes with the lid on. Set aside. (Alternatively, place the glutinous rice and coconut milk in a rice cooker and leave to cook.)

   Place the squash in a large saucepan with 1 1/2 cans of the coconut milk and 1 cup (200 g) of the brown sugar. Cook over high heat for about 10 minutes or until soft and then mash the squash. Add 1 more cup (200 g) of the brown sugar and stir over medium heat until creamy. Add the cooked rice. Stir constantly with a wooden spoon, taking care not to burn the rice. Add the remaining 1 cup (200 g) of sugar and stir constantly over medium-low heat for at least 1 hour until completely smooth and elastic. Transfer the rice mixture to a lightly greased serving platter, and spread it out evenly to 1 1/2-inch (3.5 cm) thick. Brush the top with the butter.

   To make latik, place a heavy skillet over medium-low heat. Add the remaining 1/2 cup (125 ml) of coconut milk. Stir constantly with a wooden spoon while boiling for about 20 minutes, or until the coconut milk hardens into solids and produces its own oil. The coconut solids turn brown as they are fried in their own oil. Drain the coconut oil and reserve for other use. Remove the latik and drain, then sprinkle it on top of the cake. Let the cake cool to room temperature and then cut into serving portions. The cake is easier to cut when cooled. Serve at room temperature.

Pulburon

Toasted Butter Cookies

A Spanish *polvorón* is a shortbread, but the Filipino Pulburon is a delicate, dry and powdery cookie that starts crumbling as soon as you bite into it. This unbaked cookie is made of toasted flour, powdered milk, butter and sugar. A special Pulburon mold makes the preparation easier but measuring spoons also work well. Pulburon cookies in various flavors and sizes have become popular *pasalubong* (gifts or souvenir items) purchased by people who visit the Philippines for friends back home.

Yields 20 cookies
Preparation time: 5 minutes
Cooking time: 20 minutes

1 1/2 cups (150 g) all-purpose flour
1 cup (100 g) powdered milk
1/2 cup (100 g) sugar
1 cup (150 g) unsalted butter, melted
Pulburon molds, to form the cookies
Cellophane or wax paper, for wrapping

Toast the flour in a heavy skillet over medium-low heat, stirring constantly in a circular motion with a wooden spoon for about five minutes or until the flour turns slightly brown. Do not burn the flour.

   Combine the toasted flour, powdered milk, sugar, and butter in a mixing bowl and mix well. If the mixture is too dry or loose, add more melted butter.

   Transfer the mixture into a plate. Press the mold onto the mixture. If not using the mold, scoop up 2 teaspoons of the mixture and then press together into a compact form. Then wrap each cookie in wax paper or cellophane (try using different colors for variety!) and twist the end as you would a candy or simply fold the edges under.

Egg Yolk Treats Yemas

A Yema is a decadent egg candy, typically eaten at fiestas and at Christmas or given to a party host as a gift. When you make these candies to give away, wrap each one in wax paper or in fancy colored cellophane as shown in the photograph. About the origin of this dish, one legend has it that the Spanish colonizers used huge amounts of egg whites to seal up cracks in church walls, and the leftover yolks were made into Yemas so they wouldn't go to waste. Yemas can be rolled into balls—the easiest and most common method—or triangles for a fancier presentation. Filipinos commonly use the leftover egg whites to make meringue cookies.

Makes about 20 candies
Preparation time: 25 minutes
Cooking time: 35 minutes

12 egg yolks
One 14-oz (410-ml) can sweetened condensed milk
1/2 cup (100 g) brown sugar sugar (for coating the balls in sugar) or 1 cup (200 g) brown sugar (for coating the balls in caramel)
1/4 cup (65 ml) water (for coating the balls in caramel)
Cellophane, for wrapping

Combine the egg yolks and condensed milk in a saucepan, preferably nonstick. Stir continuously over low heat for about 30 minutes or until firm. It should have the consistency of mashed potatoes. If you are not using a nonstick pan, the mixture is more liable to burn so it's imperative to watch it carefully. Transfer to a plate and let cool before forming into balls. Scoop out about 1 tablespoon of the mixture and shape into a small ball. Continue with the remainder of the mixture.

There are two options to coat the balls. To coat the ball with sugar, place the $^1/_2$ cup (100 g) of brown sugar in a bowl and roll the balls in the sugar to coat them. Place each candy in the middle of a cellophane square, gather up all four corners and twist together to secure. To coat the balls in caramel, pour the water into a saucepan or small skillet and bring to a boil. Reduce the heat to low and add the 1 cup (200 g) of brown sugar. Stir constantly until the syrup is caramelized or turns amber brown. Turn off the heat. Using a toothpick, dip each piece of candy in the syrup and place on a tray to cool. Wrap each ball with cellophane as described above.

> **Tip:** If you want to form the candies into triangles, stir the mixture over low heat a little longer to make it drier and firmer (this will make it easier to work with).

Sweet Banana and Jackfruit Rolls Turon Saba

Not to be confused with Spanish Turron, which is an almond nougat candy, the Filipino Turon is made by coating sliced bananas and jackfruit pieces with brown sugar, then wrapping them in spring roll wrappers and deep-frying them. The jackfruit slices may be omitted, although they give the banana rolls a juicy and aromatic sweetness.

Makes 20 rolls
Preparation time: 30 minutes
Cooking time: 20 minutes

1/2 cup (100 g) light brown sugar

10 ripe saba bananas, cut in half lengthwise (or regular bananas, cut in half lengthwise and then crosswise)

5 jackfruit bulbs, fresh, canned or frozen, thinly sliced into strips (optional)

One 16-oz (500-g) package of frozen 8-in (20-cm) spring roll wrappers (about 20 sheets), thawed

1 tablespoon water

2 cups (500 ml) oil for deep-frying (page 18)

Place the light brown sugar on a plate. Roll each banana piece in the sugar to coat it evenly. Place a coated banana segment and a slice or two of jackfruit (if using) in the center of a spring roll wrapper. Roll the bottom edge of the wrapper up and over the fruit and tuck it snugly around the fruit. Fold both ends in and continue rolling up the wrapper, then seal the edge with a little water and some of the sugar. Do the same with the rest of the fruit and the wrappers.

Heat the oil in a saucepan or wok over high heat. Use a wooden chopstick or skewer to check if the oil is hot enough. When it's hot enough, bubbles will form all around the stick. (Or use a deep-fryer thermometer to read the temperature, which should be between 350° and 375°F or 175° to 190°C when ready). Reduce the heat to medium once it reaches the desired temperature to avoid burning the oil.

Deep-fry two or three banana rolls at a time until golden and crispy. Do not overcrowd the pan. Sprinkle some sugar on top and serve hot.

Bibingka   Coconut Sponge Cakes

This local sponge cake is traditionally associated with *Simbang Gabi*—the nine-day series of dawn masses leading up to Christmas. December coincides with the rice harvest season, so Filipinos enjoy a variety of *kakanin* (native desserts made from rice) around Christmas time. There are so many ways to make this cake—one is to use glutinous rice and top each cake with a slice of salted egg and sugar. The aroma that comes from the cake reminds Filipinos of home. Surprisingly, this is a very popular dessert with foreign visitors to the Philippines.

Serves 4 to 6
Preparation time: 15 minutes
Cooking time 1 hour

3 eggs, beaten
1 cup (200 g) light brown sugar
2 cups (400 g) rice flour
3 tablespoons unsalted butter, melted
One 13 1/2-oz (400-ml) can coconut milk
1 tablespoon baking powder
1 banana leaf (optional)
2 tablespoons fresh or frozen grated coconut
1 tablespoon unsalted butter, sliced

In a mixing bowl, place the eggs, brown sugar, rice flour, butter, coconut milk and baking powder. Mix thoroughly.

Preheat the oven to 325°F (160°C).

If you're using a banana leaf, line a round baking pan (about 8 x 3-inch/20 x 7.5-cm) with the leaf (cut according to the size of the tray) and pour in the cake batter. The banana leaf adds fragrance to the cake when cooked but using it is optional as the cakes are still good without the leaf. If you're not using a banana leaf, lightly grease the pan with butter and pour in the cake batter.

To make individual cakes, line a 4-inch (10-cm) wide and 2 1/4-inch (5.5-cm) deep minipan with 5-inch (12.5-cm) banana leaf (this is optional) and pour batter into the minipan.

Bake for about 1 hour or until browned or a toothpick inserted near the center comes out clean. Place the cake onto a serving platter and put butter on top of the cake. Sprinkle the grated coconut on the cake.

Halo-halo

Mixed Fruits and Shaved Ice Parfait

The quintessential Halo-halo (literally mix-mix) dessert is a mixture of shaved ice, milk, various fruits, sweet beans and a topping of either Filipino Leche Flan (page 108) or Sweet Purple Yam Pudding (page 99). A "special order" means a topping of ice cream! It is normally served in a tall glass and eaten with a long spoon like a parfait. This recipe contains the standard ingredients but there are no rules what to put into Halo-halo or which item goes in first. Try sweetened red beans (sold in bottles in Asian grocery stores), *nata de coco* (coconut gelatin) or any ripe fruit. There is one rule though—mix everything up when eating.

In 4 tall parfait glasses or bowls, place a few slices of jackfruit and banana and 1 tablespoon each of two or three of the other ingredients (see list to the right). Fill each glass with 1 cup (200 g) of the crushed ice (prepare crushed ice by using either a blender or food processor) and pour the evaporated milk over the ice, dividing it evenly among the glasses. Top each glass with 1 tablespoon of the toasted young rice (if using), and then with 1 tablespoon of the Sweet Purple Yam Pudding or Filipino Leche Flan or 1 scoop of ice cream.

Serves 4
Preparation time: 15 minutes

4 bulbs fresh, frozen or canned jackfruit, sliced
1 ripe regular banana or saba banana, sliced
1 tablespoon each of 2 or 3 of the following:
 bottled coconut sport strings
 canned sweetened kidney beans
 canned sweetened chickpeas
 canned cooked corn kernels
 other commonly available fruits (canned or fresh) like lychees, mangoes or fruit cocktail
4 cups (800 g) crushed ice
2 cups (500 ml) evaporated milk (or fresh milk)
4 tablespoons toasted young rice (pinipig) or crispy rice cereal (optional)
4 tablespoons Sweet Purple Yam Pudding (page 99) or Filipino Leche Flan (page 108) or 4 scoops ice cream, any flavor

Filipino Hot Chocolate

This aromatic and easy-to-make drink reminds me of Christmas. Native cacao tablets, called *tableas*, which are made of ground cocoa beans, are simmered in water buffalo milk. Ground peanuts are added for flavor and the eggs make the drink foamy and rich. The chocolate is thickened vigorously with a wooden whisk (*batidor* or *molinillo*). If you cannot find Filipino or Mexican chocolate tablets, Hershey's® Cocoa is a good substitute.

Heat the milk in a saucepan over medium heat and add the chocolate tablets (or powder and sugar) and ground peanuts, stirring with a wooden spoon continuously until the chocolate is melted and thoroughly mixed. Add the egg yolks, if using, and mix for about 3 minutes or until thick. Serve hot.

Serves 4
Preparation time: 5 minutes
Cooking time: 3 minutes

4 cups (1 liter) milk
4 sweetened Filipino or Mexican chocolate tablets (or 4 tablespoons Hershey's® Cocoa plus 4 tablespoons of light brown sugar)
2 tablespoons peanut, peeled, toasted and finely ground (optional)
2 egg yolks, beaten (optional)

Rice Cakes with Sweet Coconut Filling Suman Bulagta

Suman is found everywhere in the Philippines—if there is a church, there is a suman vendor. There are countless varieties of this dish with almost every town or locality having its own version. Banana leaves impart a sweet aroma and taste, and a subtle color. If the leaf tears or cracks while wrapping, double wrap it with another leaf or aluminum foil rather than starting all over again with a new leaf. If banana leaves are not available, wrap the cakes in parchment paper first then in aluminum foil. It is best to eat the suman within a couple of days although they can be stored in the refrigerator for a week. To reheat them, place in a microwave (remove the foil first) for fifteen seconds with the banana leaves on, or you can heat them in a steamer for about five minutes. Don't unwrap them until just before eating, otherwise the cakes become hard and dry.

Wash the glutinous rice and drain. Leave to soak in water in a bowl for at least 1 hour. Rinse and drain through a fine sieve. Return the drained rice to the bowl.

To extract the green color from the banana leaves, place a couple of thin strips and 2 tablespoons of warm water in a mortar and mash with the pestle. Strain and pour the green liquid over the rice and mix well. Discard the banana strips.

Place the softened banana leaf on a clean surface, lighter side up, and fill the center of each leaf with 1 to 1 1/2 tablespoons of the rice mixture. Do not overfill. Fold the left and right sides of the leaf over the mixture, then fold the bottom and top over it to form a suman square packet. Place the packet folded-sides down on a clean surface while wrapping the other. Put two packets together and tie with kitchen twine. Continue with the remainder of the rice mixture.

Pour water into a stockpot and bring to a boil. Add the packets and cook over high heat for 1 hour. Completely submerge the packets by putting a heavy object over the lid, or occasionally turn the packets while boiling. When cooked, drain immediately. Open the leaf wrappings, place on individual serving plates and sprinkle with sugar and grated coconut. Or serve the unwrapped sumans in a large plate, and the sugar and coconut in another.

Makes about 15
Preparation time: 1 hour soaking time + 30 minutes
Cooking time: 1 hour

3 cups (600 g) uncooked glutinous rice
15 sheets 10-in (25-cm) squares banana leaves, rinsed with boiling water to soften
2 tablespoons warm water
Kitchen twine
10 cups (2.5 liters) water
1 cup (200 g) light brown sugar
1 cup (200 g) fresh or frozen grated coconut

Iced Tapioca Pearl and Jelly Drink

Sago at Gulaman

This sweet, thirst-quenching drink is popular during the sizzling summer months. In restaurants, it's served in a fancy glass with a spoon and a straw; street vendors serve it in a plastic cup or bag with a straw. Agar-agar or *gulaman* is used to make the jellies. Gelatin powder can also be used.

Serves 4 to 6
Preparation time: 30 minutes

8 cups (2 liters) water
1 bar white agar-agar, flaked (or 1 tablespoon gelatin powder)
1 1/2 cups (300 g) dark brown sugar
1/2 cup (50 g) dried tapioca pearls, boiled (to yield 2 cups/200 g)
Ice cubes

To make the jelly, bring 2 cups (500 ml) of the water to a boil in a saucepan. Add the agar-agar flakes and stir constantly over low heat until flakes are completely melted (if using gelatin powder, stir until the powder is completely dissolved). Transfer to a tray or baking dish and set aside to cool at room temperature. When cooled, it should be firm. Cut into small dice using a knife.

To make the sugar syrup, bring the remaining 6 cups (1.5 liters) of water to a boil in a saucepan. Add the sugar and stir constantly over medium heat for 5 minutes. Set aside to cool.

Place the cooked tapioca pearls and jelly in glasses. Pour the syrup into the glasses and top with ice cubes as desired.

Sweet Mango Juice

Serves 4
Preparation time: 15 minutes

1¹/₂ lbs (700 g) ripe mangoes, peeled
  and sliced
2 cups (250 g) ice cubes
2 cups (500 ml) water
1 tablespoon sugar (or adjust to taste)

Often called the king of fruits in the Philippines, the mango is a highly nutritious fruit that is native to India. Sweet Mango Juice is one of the best-loved drinks in the Philippines because of its smooth texture.

Combine the mango slices, ice cubes, water and sugar in a blender. Process until smooth. Serve.

Tangy Green Mango Juice

Serves 4
Preparation time: 15 minutes

1¹/₂ lbs (700 g) unripe mangoes,
  peeled and sliced
2 cups (250 g) ice cubes
2 cups (500 ml) water
1 cup (200 g) sugar (or adjust to taste)

Green mangoes can make a delicious juice but you need to add a lot of sugar. This recipe calls for 1 cup (200 g) of sugar but feel free to adjust the amount. Though don't add too much—you don't want to kill off the naturally tart taste. This tangy and invigorating drink provides a refreshing break from the heat. Filipino mangoes are green when unripe but, depending on the variety, the color as well as size may vary and some mangoes are already ripe when still green. The produce manager at your store can help you to identify the right variety.

Combine the mango slices, ice cubes, water and sugar in a blender. Process until smooth. Serve.

Healthy Ginger Tea   Salabat

Serves 4 to 6
Preparation time: 5 minutes
Cooking time: 20 minutes

1 lb (500 g) fresh ginger, peeled and
  sliced
6 cups (1.5 liters) water
1 cup (200 g) light brown sugar

This healthy ginger tea is often enjoyed during the Christmas season when it is slightly cooler than usual. With ginger's medicinal qualities, this tea warms up the body and drives away colds. In the Philippines, when a child has a sore throat, he is given a cup of warm ginger tea.

In a saucepan, combine the ginger, water, and brown sugar and bring to a boil. Cook over medium heat for 20 minutes. If the taste is too strong, add more water.

Strain the tea into a teapot. Discard the ginger. Serve hot in tea cups.

Filipino Leche Flan

Variations on this popular dessert are found in many countries but the Filipino version is sweeter than most. Just the egg yolks are used in this flan, which gives it a creamier taste and melt-in-the-mouth texture compared to versions that use whole eggs. If you prefer a less creamy, but sweeter flan, reduce the amount of sugar in the flan (the sugar in the caramel, however, should not be reduced). The flan needs to chill in the refrigerator for at least six hours before serving, so it is a good idea to make this ahead of time. Leftover flan is great addition to Halo-halo (page 104). Filipinos commonly use the leftover egg whites to make meringue cookies.

Serves 6 to 8
Preparation time: 10 minutes
  + 2 hours cooling time
Cooking time: 30 minutes

Individual flan molds (or two 9 x 2-in/23 x 5-cm flan molds or llanera)
One 12-oz (354 ml) can evaporated milk (or whole milk)
One 14-oz (410 ml) can sweetened condensed milk
1/2 cup (100 g) sugar
1/4 teaspoon vanilla extract
12 egg yolks, beaten

Caramel
3 tablespoons water
1 cup (150 g) light brown sugar

To make the Caramel, bring the water to a boil in a saucepan and reduce the heat to low before adding the sugar. Stir continuously for about 2 minutes or until the sugar caramelizes or turns amber. Immediately pour the caramelized sugar into the individual flan molds (Filipinos prefer the bigger 9 x 2-in/23 x 5-cm flan molds). Swirl the flan molds to evenly spread the caramel. Set the molds aside.

Prepare the steamer. Place a steamer in a large saucepan or work. Pour in water to just below the steamer and bring to a boil.

Combine the evaporated milk, condensed milk, sugar and vanilla extract in a bowl. Gently pass the beaten egg yolks through a strainer into the bowl. Mix thoroughly.

Pour the mixture into the flan molds containing the caramel. Cover the molds with aluminum foil, arrange the molds in the steamer (water should already be boiling before placing the molds inside the steamer) and steam for about 30 minutes. Set aside to cool and then refrigerate for at least 2 hours.

To serve, run a knife along the edges of the flan molds to loosen the flan. To remove individual flans, turn the molds over onto a platter or individual plates. To remove the larger flans, place a platter on top of the mold and, holding the platter tightly to the mold, quickly turn upside down. The flan should come out easily with the caramel on top.

How to Make Leche Flan

1 Combine the evaporated milk, condensed milk, sugar and vanilla extract.

2 Pass the beaten egg yolks through a strainer.

3 Pour the caramelized sugar into the flan molds and swirl to evenly spread the caramel.

4 Pour the flan mixture into the molds on top of the caramel.

5 Cover the molds with foil and steam for 30 minutes or until firm.

Index

The Tuttle Story
"Books to Span the East and West"

Most people are surprised when they learn that the world's largest publisher of books on Asia had its humble beginnings in the tiny American state of Vermont. The company's founder, Charles Tuttle, came from a New England family steeped in publishing, and his first love was books—especially old and rare editions.

Tuttle's father was a noted antiquarian dealer in Rutland, Vermont. Young Charles honed his knowledge of the trade working in the family bookstore, and later in the rare books section of Columbia University Library. His passion for beautiful books—old and new—never wavered through his long career as a bookseller and publisher.

After graduating from Harvard, Tuttle enlisted in the military and in 1945 was sent to Tokyo to work on General Douglas MacArthur's staff. He was tasked with helping to revive the Japanese publishing industry, which had been utterly devastated by the war. After his tour of duty was completed, he left the military, married a talented and beautiful singer, Reiko Chiba, and in 1948 began several successful business ventures.

To his astonishment, Tuttle discovered that postwar Tokyo was actually a book-lover's paradise. He befriended dealers in the Kanda district and began supplying rare Japanese editions to American libraries. He also imported American books to sell to the thousands of GIs stationed in Japan. By 1949, Tuttle's business was thriving, and he opened Tokyo's very first English-language bookstore in the Takashimaya Department Store in Ginza, to great success. Two years later, he began publishing books to fulfill the growing interest of foreigners in all things Asian.

Though a westerner, Tuttle was hugely instrumental in bringing a knowledge of Japan and Asia to a world hungry for information about the East. By the time of his death in 1993, he had published over 6,000 books on Asian culture, history and art—a legacy honored by Emperor Hirohito in 1983 with the "Order of the Sacred Treasure," the highest honor Japan bestows upon non-Japanese.

The Tuttle company today maintains an active backlist of some 1,500 titles, many of which have been continuously in print since the 1950s and 1960s—a great testament to Charles Tuttle's skill as a publisher. More than 60 years after its founding, Tuttle Publishing is more active today than at any time in its history, still inspired by Charles Tuttle's core mission—to publish fine books to span the East and West and provide a greater understanding of each.

To Ronald

Published by Tuttle Publishing, an imprint of Periplus Editions (HK) Ltd., **www.tuttlepublishing.com**

Copyright © 2010 Miki Garcia

Library of Congress Cataloging-in-Publication Data
Garcia, Miki, 1969-
  Filipino cooking / Miki Garcia ; photography by Luca Invernizzi Tettoni. —1st ed.
     p. cm.
    Includes index.
    ISBN 978-0-8048-4088-0 (hardcover)
    1. Cookery, Philippine. I. Title.
     TX724.5.P5G37 2010
     641.59599—dc22

             2009033442

ISBN 978-0-8048-4088-0 (hardcover)

Distributed by

North America, Latin America & Europe
Tuttle Publishing
364 Innovation Drive, North Clarendon, VT 05759-9436 U.S.A.
Tel: 1 (802) 773-8930; Fax: 1 (802) 773-6993
info@tuttlepublishing.com
www.tuttlepublishing.com

Asia Pacific
Berkeley Books Pte. Ltd.
61 Tai Seng Avenue #02-12, Singapore 534167
Tel: (65) 6280-1330; Fax: (65) 6280-6290
inquiries@periplus.com.sg
www.periplus.com

First edition
15 14 13 12   6 5 4 3 2
Printed in Singapore   1204CP

TUTTLE PUBLISHING® is a registered trademark of Tuttle Publishing, a division of Periplus Editions (HK) Ltd.

Resources

PilipinoMart
Offers wholesale discounts, requires no membership fee nor minimum order.
Email: info@pilipinomart.com
Tel: (626) 262 4403
www.pilipinomart.com

Filgoods International
Offers dried, bottled and canned goods.
Email: filgoods@filgoods.com
www.filgoods.com

PinoyGrocery.Com
Offers Filipino, Vietnamese and Thai products. Ships products except frozen and fresh goods.
11 South Mason Road Suite 116
Katy Texas, 77450
Email: Inquiries@PinoyGrocery.com
Tel: (281) 829 9798
www.pinoygrocery.com

Filipino Store
Offers dried goods, canned products and noodles. Frozen goods for pick-up only.
1105 E Jackson PL, Indianola, IA 50125
Email: dwightbenilda@filipino-store.com
Tel: (515) 285 3894
www.filipino-store.com

Oriental Super-Mart
A South Florida store that offers a large selection of Filipino and other Asian products including dry and frozen foods, and beverages.
5422 W. Atlantic Blvd., Margate, FL 33063
954-970-8868
orientalsupermrk@bellsouth.net
www.orientalsuper-mart.com/ourstore/

Manila Grocery Company
No online shopping but can arrange shipment of orders except frozen items.
8002 N Oak Trafficway Suite 108
Kansas City, MO 64118-1272
Email: manilagrocery@sbcglobal.net
Tel: (866) 508-8898
www.manilagroceryco.com

Philippine Food Corporation
Prefers wholesalers but will refer interested buyers to stores within their areas.
4529 N. Ravenswood Avenue Chicago Illinois 60640
Email: philfood@flash.net
Tel: (773) 784-7447
www.philippinefood.net

Phil-Am Merchandising, Inc.
Offers dry and frozen goods from its online and retail stores.
683 Newark Avenue, Jersey City, NJ 07306
Email: sales@philamfood.com
Tel: (201) 963-0455
www.philamfood.com

Asian Wok
Offers various products from 10 Asian countries, including the Philippines.
Tel: 1-800-300-6346
www.asianwok.com

ImportFood.com
Find substitutes for ingredients used in Filipino dishes from this online Thai store.
PO Box 2054, Issaquah, WA 98027
Email: info@importfood.com
Tel: 1-888-618-8424
www.importfood.com

Pinoy Mini Mall
A UK-based company that offers Filipino products and delivers all across Europe.
Tel: 0870-330-7430
www.pinoyminimall.co.uk

Kabayan
An online Australia-based company that offers frozen and dry Filipino products.
65 Hawthory Road, Kilsyth, 3137 Victoria Australia
sales@kabayan-online.com.au
Tel: 63 03 9725 6564
www.kabayan-online.com.au